FAMOUS (
OF GLA

FAMOUS CRICKETERS OF GLAMORGAN

DEAN HAYES

CHRISTOPHER DAVIES

First published in the United Kingdom in 1996 by
Christopher Davies (Publishers) Ltd
PO Box 403, Swansea, SA1 4YF

© Dean Hayes 1996

*All rights reserved. No part of this publication may
be reproduced, stored in a retrieval system,
or transmitted, in any form or by any means,
electronic, mechanical, photocopying, recording
or otherwise, without the prior permission of
Christopher Davies (Publishers) Ltd.*

British Library Cataloguing in Publication Data

A CIP record of this book is available from the British Library

ISBN 0 7154 0728 7

*Printed in Wales by
Gwasg Dinefwr Press
Llandybie, Carmarthenshire, SA18 3YD*

*Photographs:
Front cover:* Eddie Bates, Viv Richards, Tony Lewis Matthew Maynard.
Back cover: Hugh Morris, Bernard Hedges.

*For Elaine
with my Love*

CONTENTS

Acknowledgements	viii	Matthew Maynard	94
Introduction	ix	Jack Mercer	99
		Hugh Morris	103
Trevor Arnott	1	Len Muncer	108
Billy Bancroft	3	Jack Nash	112
Eddie Bates	6	Malcolm Nash	114
Joseph Brain	9	Rodney Ontong	118
Alan Butcher	12	Gilbert Parkhouse	121
Johnny Clay	15	Jim Pressdee	124
Phil Clift	20	Viv Richards	128
Tony Cordle	22	Norman Riches	132
Harry Creber	24	Frank Ryan	136
Dai Davies	27	Ravi Shastri	139
Emrys Davies	30	Don Shepherd	143
Haydn Davies	34	Cyril Smart	148
Roger Davis	37	Greg Thomas	151
Arnold Dyson	40	Maurice Turnbull	155
David Evans	43	Peter Walker	159
Roy Fredericks	47	Cyril Walters	163
Bernard Hedges	50	Steve Watkin	165
John Hopkins	53	Allan Watkins	168
Javed Miandad	57	Ossie Wheatley	171
Alan Jones	61	'Tal' Whittington	174
Eifion Jones	66	Wilf Wooller	177
Jeff Jones	70		
Willie Jones	74	*Appendices*	
George Lavis	78	Statistical Analysis	181
Tony Lewis	81	Top Tens	182
Jim McConnon	85	Batting Averages	184
Majid Khan	87	Bowling Averages	186
Austin Matthews	92	Wicket Keeping	187
		Selected Bibiliography	188

ACKNOWLEDGEMENTS

I AM GREATLY INDEBTED to the following for their help in the compilation of this book: Alan Wilkins, former Glamorgan, Gloucestershire and Northern Transvaal player and now a BBC sports commentator and Peter Stafford, a former Bolton League Cricket secretary.

I am also indebted for the kind assistance and help in obtaining the illustrations of Andrew Hignell, Morton Davies and last but by no means least the Glamorgan County Cricket Club.

D.H.

INTRODUCTION

Glamorgan C.C.C. and especially Welsh cricket, has a long history. Indeed, long before the formation of a County Club was contemplated, organised cricket was played in South Wales.

Cricket clubs had been formed at Newport (1820s), Abergavenny (1834), Llanelli (1837), Neath (1844), Cardiff (1845), Maesteg (1946) and Swansea (1848), though perhaps it was not so competitive and had more of the carefree atmosphere of the country house, where 'gentlemen of leisure' were apt to disport themselves.

One of the leading personalities in Welsh cricket at this time was Captain Samuel George Homfray – the captain and secretary of the Newport Club. The son of the managing partner of the Tredegar Iron Works, he was keen to see the standard of club cricket in the area flourish, and decided to put his money and organisational skills into achieving these goals.

In 1855, a XXII of South Wales was assembled to challenge the All-England XI, at the Arms Park. Despite the inclusion of Henry Grace and Hinkly of Kent, the South Wales side lost by five wickets, but at least it gave Homfray a clear indication of how to achieve his aim.

In September 1858, the All-England XI played XXII of Monmouthshire at Newport. It prompted 'Lillywhite's Guide' to comment: 'Homfray could not possibly pass a season unless he had some talented cricketers to entertain.' Amongst these talented cricketers were Nottinghamshire's renowned batsman, George Parr, 'the father of overarm bowling' Kent's Edgar Willsher and H. H. Stephenson, the captain of the first England team to Australia in 1861-62. There were sizeable attendances at these exhibition matches and so following this success, Homfray began to consider the formation of a team to represent South Wales. Having gained the support of a number of leading cricketers in the area, he formed the South Wales Cricket Club. It was not a successful start, for the S.W.C.C. lost by 114 runs in their opening match against the Clifton Club of Bristol. However, the return fixture at Newport a month later, saw a victory for the S.W.C.C. and Homfray won his £50 wager!

The following year, Homfray arranged five games. The game with The Knickerbockers at Aldershot saw Samuel France, the Yorkshire-born professional from Llandovery taking 11 for 84 as the S.W.C.C. ran out victors. The season established a pattern that became the norm for the club over the next few years. Most of the S.W.C.C.'s team were composed of gentlemen who had learnt their cricket at the public schools of England and were now successful businessmen in South Wales, together with the more talented cricketers of the local gentry who could afford to take the time off work to play in these two-day games.

Perhaps the most famous amateur to turn out for the S.W.C.C. was W. G. Grace, who had turned out as an 11-year-old for Clifton in the Welsh club's opening fixture. His brother E. M. Grace appeared regularly for the S.W.C.C. in the early 1860s and it was he who was responsible for W.G. appearing in the side. W.G. scored 5 and 38 against the Surrey Club and Ground and then 170 and 56 not out at Brighton!

The leading Welsh member of the S.W.C.C. was John Talbot Dillwyn Llewellyn, who was known to all as 'J.T.D.'. He was a J.P. for Carmarthenshire and had many connections in West Wales. He used these to arrange a two-day game between a Glamorganshire XI and Carmarthenshire on 5th and 6th August 1861. Though it was the first side to carry the County's game, it wasn't representative of the entire area. The wicket at Llanelli was in a terrible state after heavy rain in the days leading up to the game and so consequently, the game was a low scoring affair. Glamorgan had a 36-run lead on first innings and O'Donoghue claimed six wickets in Carmarthenshire's second innings to leave Llewellyn's side a modest target of 49. But, the wicket had cut up even more and Glamorgan fell four runs short. During the 1860s, regular fixtures were held with Carmarthenshire and J.T.D. had great hopes of forming a club to represent Glamorgan along the lines of the teams which had been formed in other parts of Wales. However, his hopes were dashed when Homfray and S.W.C.C. captain, John Lloyd severed their links with S.W.C.C. in 1865. The Grace family also broke off their connections with the S.W.C.C. and the club went into decline.

Therefore, it was left to J. T. D. Llewellyn (later Sir John T. D. Llewellyn, Squire of Penllergaer) who was to become the first Treasurer of Glamorgan C.C.C. to promote the game in the late 1860s and early

1870s. During the winter of 1868-69, Llewellyn made a great effort to form a County team and a meeting was held on 13th March at The Castle Hotel in Neath to discuss the feasibility of forming a County Club.

In May 1869, a trial match was held at The Gnoll, Neath, between a Glamorganshire XI and a Colts XXII, captained by William Bancroft of Swansea. Llewellyn also assembled a South Wales XII to play the M.C.C. at Lord's – it was a very successful trip, for his side won by 24 runs. He was able to arrange a series of friendlies in the first half of the next decade, one of which was against a West Gloucestershire side at Cardiff Arms Park. During this game, W.G. took six for 5 and hit a huge six off the first ball he received! In the 1874 edition of Lillywhite's Annual, J.T.D.'s team were described as 'Glamorganshire County Cricket Club' – an unusual description for his team only played two or three matches each season and had a membership of just over fifty. Llewellyn resurrected the S.W.C.C. in 1874 – they were quite successful and in 1878, they secured a fixture with the Australian tourists. The following year saw the inauguration of a knock-out competition called the 'South Wales Cricket Challenge Cup', which raised the competitive spirit in inter-club matches.

However, it led to many arguments over residential eligibility and so consequently, the competition and the S.W.C.C. itself was disbanded in the autumn of 1886. There were quite a few people who were upset at the break-up of the S.W.C.C., but many more who believed the time had now come to form a truly representative Glamorgan team. In the spring and early summer of 1888, J. P. Jones and William Bryant contacted all the officials of the clubs within the county boundaries regarding the feasibility of forming a county team. So on 6th July 1888, over 30 people gathered in a small room at the Angel Hotel, Cardiff. They were the 'old originals', most of them well-known men who had prospered in commerce and had a real love for cricket. But the club had quite a turbulent start, the first Minute books telling a story of repeated disappointments, a small income and a public that appeared to be disinterested.

At the very first meeting, it was proposed by W. E. Jones, Cardiff, seconded by T. John, Llwynypia and carried unanimously 'that this meeting approve and heartily support the formation of a County Cricket Club for Glamorgan'. Indeed, that is the actual first recorded minute. During the weeks of the autumn of 1888, many agonising moments were spent, wondering just who would agree to play them. Their anxiety was lifted early in the New Year, when Warwickshire agreed to play. Edmund David of St Fagan's skippered the Glamorgan team and elected to bat after winning the toss. At 70 for 9, it looked that a very embarrassing start would be made, but the last pair batted with great stubbornness to take the total to 136. James Lindley, the Cardiff professional bowled well to take 5 for 51, as Warwickshire were dismissed for 138. However, in their second innings, Glamorgan were bowled out for 80 and the visitors hit off the 79 runs required for the loss of just two wickets. Glamorgan registered their first-ever victory over Surrey Club and Ground at the Oval in August 1889, winning by 6 wickets.

The following season saw Herbie Morgan of Penarth C.C. hit the first century for Glamorgan, in the newly acquired game with Monmouthshire, which the County won comfortably. It was the side's only success, the other six games all ending in defeats. The summer of 1891 was much better, with two wins over Monmouthshire and a first-ever win over the M.C.C. at Lord's. The County played Gloucestershire this season and though they lost by an innings and 217 runs, the match had been arranged for publicity purposes by J. H. Brain, the Welsh Club's captain-secretary, who had represented the West County team between 1883 and 1889. He had returned to south Wales to work in the family's brewery at Cardiff, and was to become a driving force behind Glamorgan cricket at the turn of the century.

The County had their most successful season to date in 1892, winning five of their eight games. They repeated this number of victories the following summer, but there were also five defeats. The County though, were becoming increasingly dependent on good patronage and the support of wealthy tradesmen and businessmen. The financial reserves were falling and the public support dwindling, and there was talk of the Club being disbanded once again. In 1894, the side only won two of their seven matches and struggled to find the right combination of players. It was agreed that standards needed to be raised and eventually the committee hired Billy Bancroft for the sum of £2 a week for 20 weeks. His hiring led to great improvements in the playing standard and for the first time in 1895, the team went through a season without defeat.

Joseph Brain strongly believed that Glamorgan would only improve if they played in a higher standard of cricket, and preferably on a league basis. Competing in the recently formed Minor County Championship, the County registered their first success against Cornwall at St Helen's, winning by 233 runs, and went on to have a very successful first season. They ended the summer in second place, whilst in 1898, they won six of their eight games and had a sound claim to the Championship title. But, the ruling was that the title would be decided by the number of defeats! The side now possessed three outstanding players in J. H. Brain, Harry Creber and Billy Bancroft who achieved the rare feat of a century and a hat-trick in the game against Surrey II in 1899.

The following season, Glamorgan shared the title, but in 1901, they failed to maintain their progress and slipped to fifth place. However, Herbie Morgan scored 254 out of Glamorgan's total of 538 in the match against Monmouthshire – it was the highest score to date by a Glamorgan batsman.

In 1905, Brain arranged 14 games, including a match with the Australians at the Arms Park, though it was a combined XI with neighbours Monmouthshire. There were four guest players, whilst the Glamorgan stars included Bancroft, Creber, Jack Nash, Riches and Brain. But the performance of the South Wales XI was very disappointing. In fact, the 1905 season was not a successful one, the only batsman in form was Bancroft who averaged 51 – a feat which brought him a 20-guinea cheque from Sir J. T. D. Llewellyn. I suppose the lowest point of the season came at Chippenham when Wiltshire dismissed Glamorgan for just 20 runs – it remains their lowest ever total.

The County received a great blow at the end of the 1906 season, when Joseph Brain announced that he wanted to stand down from the captaincy and retire from Minor County cricket.

In 1907, there was a change to the format of the Minor County competition, with the teams divided into four regional groups, with the top sides in each division playing in an end of season knock-out competition to provide the overall winner. The side easily won their section, with Norman Riches scoring 217 against Dorset. After beating Surrey II in the semi-final, the County secured home advantage for the final with Lancashire II, but lost by 108 runs. The side were to reach the final for three consecutive seasons, only to lose on each occasion. The format of the Minor County Championship changed again in 1910, with the teams now split into two halves and the two winners meeting to find the overall champion county.

It was a disappointing season, Glamorgan finishing second to Berkshire in their section. The only bright spot was the selection of Glamorgan captain 'Tal' Whittington for the M.C.C. tour of the West Indies, where he scored 685 runs to top the averages. The following season was one of further disappointment, though Norman Riches scored 1,015 runs at an average of 92.27 to create a new County record. In the years leading up to the First World War, the county strengthened their playing staff by signing William Bestwick, the former Derbyshire fast-medium bowler, who had joined Llanelli and qualified by residence for the Welsh county and Eddie Bates who had played the occasional game for Yorkshire between 1907 and 1913.

After the hostilities of the 1914-18 War, life began to get back to normal. New and enthusiastic members were added to the Committee – they were more determined than ever to gain first-class status.

The County returned to the Minor County Championship in 1920 and though they only finished in sixth place, there were important victories over the M.C.C. and Surrey II (twice). In September of that year, the Committee discussed 'the question of entering the first-class county competition'. The Committee realised the difficulty of obtaining fixtures with eight first-class counties, but resolved that the matter should be left in the hands of 'Tal' Whittington. Given the committee's full support, he travelled the country persuading the established county clubs that Glamorgan were well fitted to enter the first-class ranks. But before the M.C.C. could sanction promotion Glamorgan, by their own personal endeavours, had to get eight county clubs to give them home and away matches.

'Tal' Whittington toiled unceasingly. Somerset agreed, then Gloucestershire, Worcestershire, Derbyshire, Leicestershire, Northants and of the more influential counties, Lancashire promised they would do all they could. In November, Whittington was able to report to the Committee that seven first-class counties had consented to give the Club fixtures. There was no going back now and the Committee requested Whittington to obtain the eighth 'at any cost whatsoever'. Sussex and Hampshire were added to the list and in 1921, Glamorgan were elevated to first-class status.

Glamorgan embarked on its big adventure, but disillusionment was soon to come, and as the economic position of South Wales deteriorated, it was a wonder that first-class cricket survived at all. The County had to rely on amateurs, many of whom were past their prime.

Indeed, it has been said Glamorgan were stronger as a Minor County club than in 1921.

Glamorgan's debut in first-class cricket was astonishing. Sussex were defeated at Cardiff on Friday 20th May 1921, by 23 runs. But, as I said, disillusionment, even among the toughest Welshmen, soon set in and only one other victory came Glamorgan's way in a season with no fewer than fourteen thrashings in eighteen matches. Wisden pronounced: 'Glamorganshire's promotion to first-class cricket was not justified ' Only captain Norman Riches made the grade; he scored 1,005 runs at an average of 41.87, but he was in his 39th year. Glamorgan's main bowlers in this distressful baptism, were Jack Nash and Harry Creber, both 47 years of age. Nash took 90 wickets at 17.34 – a remarkable record, for both he and Creber had little respite in that first year of championship cricket. The indifferent batting of the Glamorgan side did not allow for any long rests in the pavilion! An eccentric batsman in Glamorgan's ranks was J. R. Tait, who narrowly missed fame and a permanent place in Glamorgan cricket history by just failing to score a century in Glamorgan's very first match against Sussex. In Glamorgan's second innings, he had scored 96 not out at the end of the second day. The first ball he received the following morning, was a full toss on the leg-side from Maurice Tate. Under normal circumstances, 'Jock' would have swept it to the boundary, but nerves got the better of him and he was bowled a few balls later without adding to his score.

The honour of being Glamorgan's first centurion went to 'Billy' Spiller who, after making his first-class debut against Worcestershire at Kidderminster, scored a hundred in his next match against Northants at Northampton on 21st July 1921. Also, that first season saw the first appearance of a certain J. C. Clay, who bowled extremely fast or slow as the whim took him, collected 41 wickets – but more of his contribution to Glamorgan cricket later.

Finance was Glamorgan's perpetual and perplexing problem, but in September 1921, the Committee decided to take the plunge and import professionals. Mercer, Abel, Sullivan and Ryan were provisionally engaged as professionals. It marked the beginning of a new era and although Abel and Sullivan, who came from Surrey, stayed only a few seasons, the names of Jack Mercer and Frank Ryan became part of Glamorgan's history.

In 1923, the tradition began of playing the touring side on August

Bank Holiday – the custom starting with the defeat of the West Indies. The season will also go down in history as the one which produced the first native born professional in Dai Davies.

The matches against Lancashire in 1924, brought marked contrasting results for the Welsh county. In May, at Aigburth, Liverpool, Lancashire had been dismissed for 49 (Spencer 5 for 9) on a soft wicket, but Glamorgan fared even worse and were bowled out for just 22, with Cecil Parking taking 6 for 6. Lancashire won by 128 runs and that 22 remains Glamorgan's lowest all out score in the county's seventy-two years' records in first-class company. Curiously, their next lowest score was also made against Lancashire in 1958. In the return match at Swansea, both sides were dismissed on the opening day, Glamorgan for 153 and Lancashire for 151, and there was no play on the second day due to rain. The final day was full of thrills, as Lancashire chased 146 to win. At 83 for 3, they were well on course, but Ryan bringing the ball down from his fine height, took five for 11, as seven Lancashire wickets crashed for 23 runs. Glamorgan had won by 38 runs – it was probably their finest victory up to this time.

It was in 1926 that Glamorgan really settled down, for under the leadership of Clay, they were actual contenders for the Championship until the last few matches ended in disaster and brought them back to 8th in the table. Jack Bell scored 1,547 runs and was the first batsman to score a double century – 255 v. Worcestershire at Dudley. Eddie Bates passed the thousand run mark and both Jack Mercer and Frank Ryan took over a hundred wickets. In 1927, the County upset the form book with an innings victory over Nottinghamshire in the final game of that season, thereby depriving them of the Championship and presenting it by a decimal point to Lancashire. Without doubt, 1927 was Eddie Bates's, year. He opened with a century, and in the sensational match mentioned above, he played his finest innings ever to score 163. During the season, he also became the first Glamorgan player to score two centuries in a match – 105 and 111 v. Essex at Leyton. In 1929, the South African tourists were defeated at Pontypridd and Maurice Turnbull became the first Glamorgan player to win a Test cap, when he played against New Zealand at Christchurch. He was elected captain in 1930 and secretary the following year. From 1930 to 1936, the new Glamorgan was taking shape, and though there were only isolated wins in each season, the reorganisation of the County was perhaps more important than the results.

By the middle of the decade, the County had a more settled look. In 1935, an aggressive middle-order batsman by the name of Cyril Smart hit a then world record of 32 runs off a 6-ball over by Hampshire's Hill at Cardiff. Also at the Arms Park that summer, Glamorgan following on 259 runs behind the South Africans, lost their first 9 wickets on the last day for 114. Cyril Smart was joined by debutant D. W. Hughes, the pair adding 131 at a furious pace to save the match. The season saw Emrys Davies become the first Glamorgan player to perform the 'double', while Johnny Clay belatedly gained a cap for England against South Africa at the Oval.

An important event took place in 1936, and that was the amalgamation with Monmouthshire C.C.C. All Monmouthshire players became eligible for Glamorgan and indeed, some of the County's best youngsters were from Monmouthshire – Phil Croft and Allan Watkins being two examples. Also that season, Jack Mercer achieved another County record, by taking all 10 Worcestershire wickets in an innings.

Many more records were broken in 1937. The County finished 7th in the championship table – their best season to date. A lot of the success was down to J. C. Clay, who took the County record total of 176 wickets at 17.34. Other records created that season included: the highest aggregate number of runs in a season – 1,954 by Emrys Davies; three centuries in one innings, Dyson, Emrys Davies and Turnbull against Leicestershire at Leicester, whilst the latter of these three batsmen, took 49 catches, the highest number in a season.

War broke out just as Glamorgan were developing into a really fine side. In 1946, the County regrouped, finding their players, like other counties, returning from various parts of the world and war action. Clay captained the side which finished sixth in the County Championship, their highest place to date.

Wilf Wooller became captain in 1947 and also secretary of the club. The side was also strengthened by Len Muncer, the Middlesex all-rounder. It was Wooller's dynamic leadership, reflecting an inspirational team spirit, that brought the first ever County Championship victory for Glamorgan in 1948.

The Championship season started in fine fashion as the County's batsmen chased a target of 311 in 290 minutes to beat Essex at the Arms Park. Against Somerset, Clay was unavailable, so Wooller called up Neath's Stan Trick, a left-arm spinner who had made a few appearances in 1946. It proved to be an inspired move as Trick took 12 wickets to bowl the Welsh side to a 137-run victory. It was Glamorgan's 100th Championship win and put them top of the table. Willie Jones scored two double centuries (207 v. Kent and 212* v. Essex) within a fortnight, whilst in between, came two comfortable home victories. Glamorgan's lead was whittled away in July, as Derbyshire won four matches to the Welsh County's two draws and two defeats. At Weston-super-Mare, Glamorgan were dismissed for 70 on a damp wicket, Somerset gaining a first innings lead of 96. At one stage, Glamorgan's lead was only 42 with four wickets left, but some hefty hitting by Wooller, supported by Haydn Davies and Hever set Somerset 105 to win. The Welshmen rose to the occasion with Hever taking three early wickets and Muncer tying down the batsmen. Wooller led by example and took three superb catches at short-leg as Somerset struggled to 90 for 9. Uncharacteristically, Emrys Davies spilled a catch but Watkins took his chance brilliantly off the bowling of Muncer and Glamorgan had won – they were now back at the top of the table.

Their stay was short-lived, as Yorkshire defeated Worcestershire and moved into pole position with just four games to play. Glamorgan's next match was against Surrey at the Arms Park – a match that both sides knew could decide the outcome of the Championship.

A few eyebrows were raised when Wooller decided to recall the 50-year-old Clay to the side, but it was to pay dividends. Glamorgan won the toss and batted first, scoring 239, with Wooller top-scoring with 89. Surrey faced just one hour of batting before the close of the first day's play. Hever and Wooller picked up three quick wickets to leave Surrey on 22 for 3. Wooller then introduced Clay, who took three wickets in an over and along with Muncer they produced a clatter of wickets to leave Surrey on 47 for 9 at the close! Clay wrapped up the proceedings in the fourth over of the second day, enabling Wooller to invite Surrey to follow-on. Though conditions were slightly easier for batting, Surrey were dismissed for 165, to give Glamorgan victory by an innings and 24 runs – Clay had match figures of 10 for 65 and led the team off to a standing ovation. Clay was retained in the side and travelled down to Bournemouth for the game with Hampshire. It was a game that if Glamorgan won, would put Surrey's bid out of reach and with Derbyshire already out of contention, Yorkshire would need to win both of their remaining matches to clinch the title. Only ten minutes play was possible on the Saturday, and so Wooller instructed his batsmen on the Monday to get 300 runs quickly so that he could declare later in the day. Everything went according to plan as Glamorgan were bowled out for 315 by 5.30 p.m. By the close of play, Hampshire had lost six wickets! It only took thirty minutes on the final morning for the Hampshire resistance to end, being bowled out for 84. Following-on, they were dismissed a second time for 116 (Clay 6 for 48) to give Glamorgan victory by an innings and 115 runs.

A large number of Welsh supporters had travelled to Bournemouth and gathered in front of the pavilion, singing 'Mae Hen Wlad Fy Nhadau' and 'Sospan Fach' as news filtered through that Yorkshire were heading for defeat – Glamorgan had become County Champions.

The theory of concentrating on leg-side attack had brought Glamorgan their success, but after that epic year of 1948, other counties accepted the leg-side theory and the Club's fortunes varied afterwards. Allan Watkins toured South Africa with the M.C.C. in 1948-49 (Wooller had been invited, but declined the invitation because of his work in Cardiff). In the fourth Test at Johannesburg, Watkins became Glamorgan's first centurion in Test cricket.

An immediate post-war Appeal was launched by Mr. H. Merrett, raising £11,000 and by 1950, Glamorgan had acquired liquid assets of almost £30,000 – a far cry from the pre-war position.

During the winter months, the Club had acquired the services of Jim McConnon from Neath, who was seen as the ideal replacement for Clay, though it was Gilbert Parkhouse who was the star of the 1950 season. He established a series of new batting records – he hit seven centuries, including hundreds in each innings against Somerset at Cardiff and passed 1,000 runs on 17th June – the quickest ever for Glamorgan. Described by some as the most gifted batsman ever to play for the Club, he made his Test debut against West Indies at Lord's. McConnon came good the following season and performed the hat-trick at Swansea, as Glamorgan defeated the South Africans by 64 runs – the only county to beat them on that tour.

In 1952, Glamorgan after a very stormy committee meeting, started a Supporters' Club and ran football pools. These were to be very successful and true to policy, coaching schemes were spread far and wide throughout South Wales and a new indoor school opened at Neath.

In 1954, McConnon, Watkins and Wooller all took over 100 wickets with the last pair achieving the 'double', a target only achieved previously by Emrys Davies and Muncer. Shepherd, who had been failing as a fast-medium opening bowler, began to concentrate on off-breaks. During this season, he took a career-best nine for 47 as Northants were beaten by 262 runs at the Arms Park. He was to take more wickets than any other Glamorgan bowler, and in 1957 captured 168 wickets, just falling short of Clay's record.

During the early 1950s, a close-knit team spirit had been forged by the Glamorgan players with Parkhouse the mainstay of the batting, though young players like Alan Jones, Tony Lewis and Peter Walker were beginning to make their way in the game. However, morale in the dressing room dropped as the side slid down the table in 1957 as off-the-field rumours hit the local headlines. The first involved the question of the County acquiring their own ground, and during the summer, a sub-committee was formed to discuss the feasibility of Glamorgan acquiring a site on land in Sophia Gardens, Cardiff. It wasn't the only event, for Wooller, who didn't see eye to eye with some committee members was considering his playing future. There were many rows, but Wooller offered to stay on for one more season as captain, a move which spoke volumes for his commitment to Glamorgan, but the committee rejected the offer and so the Club were left without a captain for the 1959 season. On 31st October 1958, the first ever Social General Meeting of the Club was held at Bridgend Town Hall with over 350 members present. No decisions were made, but at the end of the evening, it was clear that the majority wanted Wooller to continue as captain-secretary. His re-appointment in both posts was a formality at the A.G.M. of 1959. During the winter of 1959-60, Wooller realised that his playing days were drawing to a close and informed the committee that the 1960 season would be his last.

Ossie Wheatley captained the County for six seasons from 1961, two of which were very good ones. In 1963, the team enjoyed their most successful year since 1948, finishing 2nd to Yorkshire in the County Championship. The County won 11 of their 28 matches and lost 8, this was due to the fact that as a captain, Wheatley always liked to make a good game of cricket by declaring. There were many factors behind the County's success – Alan Jones and Bernard Hedges had established themselves as top-class opening batsmen, Tony Lewis was available full-time and Jim Pressdee began to believe in himself again and achieved the 'double'. The season also saw two other landmarks in the Club's history. The first was the signing of Tony Cordle, the Club's first West Indian professional, whilst the second, was the Club's inaugural one-day match against Somerset at Cardiff, in which Bernard Hedges made a solid unbeaten 103. Also arriving on the scene was a young left-arm quick bowler by the name of Jeff Jones. In fact, Jones won his England cap before his county cap, by playing in the second Test against India at Bombay in 1963-64.

The summer of 1964 will always be remembered as the year when Glamorgan beat Australia for the first time, in a low scoring match. The Welsh side batted first and scored 197. A shower then brought the wicket to life and before the close of play on the Saturday, Pressdee and Shepherd had reduced the Australians to 39 for 6. Though the wicket became easier, Australia never recovered against Glamorgan's 'spin-twins' and brilliant catching and lost by 36 runs.

There was a welcome return to form in 1965, as the Club finished 3rd in the Championship, behind Worcestershire and Northants. The match which probably cost Glamorgan the Championship was the one against Northants at Cardiff in August. Up to the last day, Northants were in trouble and at one stage, were 32 for 6, with a lead of only 39.

Glamorgan were eventually required to get 139 for victory, but a heavy storm affected the wicket before the match could resume and Northants won by 18 runs. The following year saw Glamorgan rebuilding their team as well as their new ground at Sophia Gardens.

In 1967, Tony Lewis followed Wheatley as captain, who continued to play for a couple of seasons on a part-time basis in order to concentrate on his business commitments. Jim Pressdee had unexpectedly left for South Africa and wicket-keeper David Evans, who had followed Davies, gave way to Eifion Jones.

The Club began to show some form in 1968 and finished 3rd in the Championship, though Jeff Jones damaged shoulder ligaments in early June and had to miss the rest of the season. Worse was to come when a specialist found a mild arthritic condition in the elbow joint and though Jones tried to make a comeback, he was unable to bowl properly and had to retire prematurely from county cricket. Malcolm Nash and Tony Cordle had joined the medium-fast bowling attack, whilst the acquisition of a young Pakistani named Majid Khan had a major impact on the side. The highlight of 1968 was Glamorgan's win over Australia – the second time within four years and both at Swansea. Shepherd led the side in the absence of Lewis and on winning the toss, elected to bat. Alan Jones was in superb form and made a memorable 99, as the Welsh side totalled 224. The Australians were bowled out for 110, with Nash's controlled left-arm swing taking 5 for 28. In their second innings the Glamorgan batsmen went for quick runs and were able to set the Australians a target of 365 in 390 minutes on the last day. The only man standing in the way of another Glamorgan victory was Paul Sheahan who was in full control. He was eventually brilliantly caught and bowled by Walker for 137, enabling Glamorgan to run out winners by 79 runs. In 1969, Tony Lewis led Glamorgan to another Championship success. The County was undefeated in 24 games – the last side to achieve as much was Lancashire in 1930.

The secret of Glamorgan's success was 'hard work and happiness' and all thirteen players, a remarkably small number, played an important part in one match or another. The batting was an improvement upon that of the 1948 side and much of this can be traced to the two overseas players, Majid Khan and Bryan Davies. Majid was in a class of his own with magnificent style and power. His 147 against the West Indies and 156 against Worcestershire were two of the best innings of the summer. On the bowling front, Shepherd celebrated his 2,000th victim whilst Cordle took nine for 49 against Leicestershire at Colwyn Bay. All the side fielded well and this was proved by Wheatley's swift and accurate return that brought about the running-out of John Lever with the last ball of a memorable Essex match to give Glamorgan victory by 1 run.

At the end of the season, Glamorgan were honoured by the appointment of Lewis as captain of M.C.C.'s touring team to the Far East, whilst Alan Jones and Don Shepherd were also selected.

In 1970, the County finished 2nd to Kent, but thereafter things began to go wrong. The 50th year of first-class cricket for the Welsh club was not a happy one and the committee realised that the Championship-winning squad was beginning to break up.

Tony Lewis told the committee that he wanted to step down from the captaincy at the end of the 1972 season. On 20th December 1972, he became the first Glamorgan player to captain England in Test cricket by leading out the side for the first Test at the Feroz Shah Kotla ground in Delhi – he later hit his maiden Test century in the fourth Test at Kanpur.

In 1973, Majid Khan was made captain, but he was too pleasant a man to captain a county side that needed re-structuring and discipline. The team began to fall back to the lower reaches of the Championship table and in 1976 finished bottom of the table for the first time since 1929. The members once again demanded an Extraordinary General Meeting. Not only were they upset at the performances on the field of play, but also with the controversial resignations of Majid Khan and Roger Davies in mid-season.

Alan Jones captained the side for the next two seasons and had his moment of glory by taking Glamorgan to Lord's for the Gillette Cup Final in 1977, where they lost to Middlesex amidst great excitement for the many thousands of Welsh supporters who had made the journey. In 1979, Robin Hobbs, the former Essex and England leg-spinner took over the captaincy, but he had retired some four years earlier and found the task of returning to first-class cricket a difficult one. Malcolm Nash replaced him in 1980, but in 1982, the captaincy switched to Javed Miandad, who had joined the Club from Sussex. It changed hands again in mid-season when Barry Lloyd took over. At the end of the 1982 season, the Club signed Mike Selvey, the former Middlesex and England bowler, thus becoming the County's seventh captain in the space of the last eight years. At the close of the 1983 season, Alan Jones retired to take over as full-time coach from Tom Cartwright and David Lewis became Chairman of the Cricket Committee and things began to look up.

The now experienced Rodney Ontong took over the captaincy and concentrated on off-spin instead of his medium-pace. He was well supported by the much needed slow left-arm spin of John Steele, who had joined the Club from Leicestershire and for the first time since 1969, Glamorgan were unbeaten at home in the Championship.

By 1985, the Glamorgan side had improved tremendously. Alan Lewis Jones and John Hopkins were solid, reliable openers, followed by Ontong, Miandad (now a world-class player and available full-time), Younis Ahmed, and two young players in Hugh Morris and Matthew Maynard, who hit a debut century against Yorkshire. The team also possessed a pair of young Welsh opening bowlers in Steve Barwick and Greg Thomas, who was regarded as 'the fastest white man in county cricket'.

There was a sorry start to the 1986 season. Ontong felt the side lacked an overseas fast bowler and told the committee that he would only lead the side again if one was signed. The officials sympathised with him and Ezra Moseley was signed with the intention of playing in certain midweek Championship games and Miandad playing in the rest. This upset Javed, who didn't relish playing on a rota basis again, and he said he would prefer not to play at all unless the County offered him a three-year contract. The Club's officials couldn't realistically agree to these demands and told Miandad to be available for the 1986 season, during which they would review his future with the Club. This did not happen and he parted company with the County.

Rodney Ontong found that his role as captain was putting increased pressure on his game and told David Lewis that he didn't want to lead the side in 1987. In fact, he stood down for the second half of the 1986 season and was the first to pledge his support to the 22-year-old Hugh Morris, who became the Club's youngest ever captain.

The Club had one of its strongest playing staff for years in 1987 and rose from 17th place the previous summer to 13th. They could, without the spate of injuries they suffered, have finished higher, but even so, many people were suggesting that the Club were finally on the verge of a new era of success.

Glamorgan celebrated their 100th birthday by having their best ever season in one-day cricket, yet finished 17th in the County Championship – the same position they occupied in their first year in the competition some 67 years earlier. The Club endured another disappointing summer in 1989, but the following year rose to 8th in the County Championship. This was due in the main to four batsmen: Viv Richards 1,425 runs (61.95) Alan Butcher 2,044 runs (60.11) Hugh Morris 1,914 runs (51.72) and Matthew Maynard 1,306 runs (45.03).

After two mediocre summers, there is no doubt that pride of place for the 1993 domestic season must go to Glamorgan. Putting an early defeat in the Benson and Hedges Cup quickly behind them, the County emerged as potential winners of all three other competitions, until losing a Nat-West semi-final they should have won.

Their drive for the County Championship, where they eventually finished third was interrupted when for the first time the selectors deprived the County of two players for the same England team. Further compliments followed when five Glamorgan players (Maynard, Watkin, Morris, Croft and Dale) were selected for the winter tours despite the omission of Colin Metson, probably the best wicket-keeper in the country.

The County's new-found faithful made their pilgrimage to Canterbury for the equivalent of a third one-day final when the Welshmen eventually lifted the inaugural and multicoloured AXA Equity and Law Sunday League, that fortuitously had the two joint leaders scheduled to meet each other in the last match.

A new maturity is evident in some of the younger players, of whom Tony Cottey, Adrian Dale and Robert Croft are growing into class players. Formerly under the personable and exemplary leadership of Hugh Morris and now about to continue under Matthew Maynard's captaincy, a strong unifying force is at work within the Welsh county. It should come as no surprise if further honours come their way.

Since Glamorgan became a first-class county, they have produced several fine sides and considerably more outstanding cricketers than the majority of the county clubs. This book I hope, captures the flavour of those players.

Dean Hayes
Bamber Bridge
September, 1995

TREVOR ARNOTT

Born: 16th February 1902. Radyr
Died: 2nd February, 1975
Played: 1921-1930

FIRST-CLASS GLAMORGAN RECORD

Innings	Not Out	Runs	H.Sc.	Average	100's
321	25	4726	153	15.96	3

Overs	Mdns	Runs	Wkts	Average	Best
3697.3	642	11435	361	31.68	7-40

NOTABLE FEATS

- He performed the first Championship hat-trick for Glamorgan in the match v. Somerset at the Arms Park in 1926.

TREVOR ARNOTT was a hard-hitting batsman with several spectacular Championship centuries to his credit, and as a fast-medium bowler he took almost 400 wickets.

It was towards the end of the 1920 season when Radyr-born Trevor Arnott, then a 19-year-old all-rounder from Wycliffe School, agreed to play for Glamorgan, after impressing in a Colts trial.

He made his debut for the county in the first season first-class status was attained and until 1930 served the County well – his value was beyond price in the early days. As a bowler, his best season was 1923, when he took 64 wickets at 24.28 each, including a fine display of seam bowling that saw him take seven for 40 as the West Indies were dismissed for 201.

His maiden century against Derbyshire the following season only occupied 75 minutes and included a number of bold strokes. Indeed, the way he went to his hundred typified his cavalier approach to batting. His score stood at 96 as Norman Riches went down the wicket to give the young all-rounder a word of advice: 'Now Trevor,' he said, 'don't be rash. Get these four runs in singles.' But Arnott responded by smashing the next ball he faced onto the roof of the rugby grandstand! The summer of 1926 was a season in which his worth with the ball was shown. He took the first Championship hat-trick for the Welsh team. It came in the match with Somerset as the visitors were dismissed for 59 on a damp Arms Park wicket. He caused a quick collapse against Warwickshire, taking the first four wickets before the total had reached 35. He had a good game with the bat against Gloucestershire, hitting 63 out of 80 runs added by the last three wickets, after the Welsh side had struggled to 63 for seven. Needing 119 runs to win, Glamorgan collapsed before some hard-hitting by Arnott turned the scales. Against Worcestershire, he and Bell shared in a hurricane partnership of 166 in seventy minutes, before Arnott was dismissed for 87.

In 1927, he opened the Gentleman's batting with L. G. Crawley at Scarborough, and among his tours were those to the U.S.A. with Incognito, West Indies with Lord Tennyson's team and Argentina with Sir Julien Cahn's team.

That summer of 1927 saw Arnott make his second first-class century. Against Surrey at the Oval, the County lost by 37 runs after having been set 413 for victory. This fine effort was mainly due to Trevor Arnott who played an invaluable innings of 126.

In 1928, he succeeded Clay as captain of the Club. Despite all the departures and resignations, Arnott's team won the first game of the season beating Worcestershire at the Arms Park by 33 runs. Arnott hit the highest score of his career, 153, in the match against Essex at Swansea. He played a captain's role by toiling away for long spells, but by now he lacked penetration, and though he ended the season with 60 wickets, they cost him 39.73 runs each. It was also a season in which he set a new Glamorgan record for having the most runs scored off his bowling, when he took three for 213 (0 for 92 and 3 for 121) against Sussex at Eastbourne.

Ever proud at his County, Trevor Arnott enjoyed recalling a remark made by Lord Harris to him at a captain's meeting at Lord's: 'You are fortunate indeed to be in the First Division!' He replied humbly: 'Maybe one day we shall win it.' No-one had greater pleasure from Glamorgan's 1948 and 1969 Championships than Trevor Arnott.

He died at Ross-on-Wye on February 2nd 1975, a fortnight before his 73rd birthday. His services to Glamorgan cricket can never be over-estimated and when he finally retired in 1930, the County missed the genial giant who so often rebelled against the obvious and the orthodox.

BILLY BANCROFT

Born: 2nd March, 1871. Swansea
Died: 3rd March, 1959
Played: 1889-1914

GLAMORGAN RECORD

Innings	Not Out	Runs	H.Sc.	Average	100's
358	20	8353	157	24.71	7

Overs	Mdns	Runs	Wkts	Average	Best
44.1	12	153	9	17.00	3-30

NOTABLE FEATS
- In 1899, he achieved the rare feat of taking a hat-trick and scoring a century v. Surrey II.
- He was the County's first professional cricketer.
- He was a rugby international, playing in 33 successive International matches at full-back for Wales.

A MEMBER OF A well-known sporting family, Billy Bancroft was brought up in a cottage alongside the St Helen's ground at Swansea. His grandfather was the Swansea professional and led the Colts XXII against Llewelyn's Glamorganshire team in 1869.

– *Famous Cricketers of Glamorgan* –

Billy Bancroft seated first left; T. A. L. Whittington seated centre.

Billy's father was also a useful player for Swansea and the South Wales Cricket Club, and they both appeared for Glamorgan in the trial match against the Colts XXI in 1892. Billy Bancroft was one of the Club's leading professionals during the minor county era, scoring over 8,000 runs in a career between 1889 and 1914.

In 1891, Glamorgan had their first-ever win at Lord's over the M.C.C. Glamorgan batted first and scored 218, with Billy Bancroft top scoring with 56, as his side went on to win the match by 18 runs.

The Swansea cricketer was also a rugby international, playing in 33 successive International matches at full-back for Wales. Winning his first cap at the age of 18 and the last in 1901, he claimed to have taken every penalty and every place-kick for his country in that time. A fine kicker, he scored over 1,000 points in his career, 1895-1901, with Swansea Rugby Football Club.

At the end of the 1894 season, it was agreed that the time had come to raise standards by engaging a professional. Several names were discussed, but eventually, Billy Bancroft was hired and became the County's first professional for the sum of £2 a week for twenty weeks. Although it meant a greater financial commitment for the County, Bancroft's hiring led to Glamorgan going through the 1895 season without a defeat. However, Bancroft's appointment did put even greater pressure on the Club's already limited finances, so Joseph Brain had to organise several friendly matches in an attempt to boost funds.

The following summer, Glamorgan were set 211 to win by Monmouthshire and looked in quite a hopeless position when they lost five early wickets. However, Billy Bancroft got his head down to make a brilliant 119 and led the county to a two-wicket win. Both he and Brain began to instill a feeling of greater confidence and a much more professional attitude, and in 1897, Bancroft top scored in the match against Cornwall, with a second innings 'knock' of 71 as Glamorgan won by 233 runs – it was the County's first victory in the Minor County Championship.

In 1899, Bancroft began to emerge as a fine all-rounder and in the match against Surrey II, he achieved the rare feat of taking a hat-trick and scoring a century. In fact, on the odd occasions when the Club were struggling to raise a side, he also kept wicket. The following year, Glamorgan ended on top of the table along with Durham and Northamptonshire as the title was shared. The County won six matches that season, including two over Surrey II, in which Bancroft hit a forceful 65 – Glamorgan totalled 388 in the match at the Oval – the title success was as a result of all the hard work Bancroft and Brain had put in.

In 1905, Bancroft was the only Glamorgan batsman in form and averaged around 51 – it was a feat which brought him a 20-guinea cheque from Sir John Llewelyn, who had always been one of his most ardent admirers. It was not until 1896, that Billy Bancroft was appointed groundsman at St Helen's, and only then that the Club paid any serious attention to the square. At the turn of the century, a groundsman's cottage was built in the south-western corner of the ground and it became the home of the Bancroft family. Billy Bancroft acted as caretaker-cum-groundsman, part of his duties including the running of the nets and practice sessions.

Bancroft kept his association with the St Helen's ground even after he retired and in the period between the wars, acted as steward in the members enclosure, often sitting at the bottom of the pavilion steps, completely engrossed in the game – a small figure, with the inevitable flower in his button hole – and always willing to pass on advice. Players famous and not so famous always had a cheery word for Billy Bancroft as they passed him at the foot of the eighty-four steps which led from the Swansea pavilion to the cricket field.

Billy also coached many youngsters, including Gilbert Parkhouse. As a boy, Gilbert in knickerbockers would delight in taking a bat and it is said that even as young as he was, he was a natural little cricketer. Spotted by Bancroft, a personal association between the veteran and the schoolboy developed. At every opportunity, Billy would be at the nets showing the schoolboy the way it should be done. It was Bancroft's own admission that one of his proudest sporting moments came in the 1950s when Parkhouse played for England.

Billy Bancroft died in Swansea on 3rd March 1959, the day after his 88th birthday.

There is no doubt that without the all-round services of Billy Bancroft the Club would not have survived very far into the twentieth century.

EDDIE BATES

Born: 5th March, 1884. Kirkheaton, Yorkshire
Died: 17th January, 1957
Played: 1920-1931

FIRST-CLASS GLAMORGAN RECORD

Innings	Not Out	Runs	H.Sc.	Average	100's
510	15	12802	200*	25.86	10

Overs	Mdns	Runs	Wkts	Average	Best
2217.4	213	8707	239	36.43	8-93

NOTABLE FEATS
- He scored 200* v. Worcestershire at Kidderminster in 1927.
- He scored 105 and 111 v. Essex at Leyton in 1927.
- He scored 1,000 runs in a season for Glamorgan on 7 occasions.
- In 1928, he held 5 catches in an innings during the match v. Warwickshire at Edgbaston.

Eddie Bates was a stocky batsman and occasional leg-spinner who played for Yorkshire between 1907 and 1913. He couldn't secure a regular place in the Yorkshire side, as did his more famous 'Billy' Bates, and so decided to try his luck in the South Wales Leagues and qualify for Glamorgan.

There is no doubt that he brought with him a certain toughness acquired from the hard school of the Yorkshire Leagues.

On his arrival in South Wales he was dubbed 'The Marquis' as he possessed a fine wardrobe. In fact, he was once described as being 'not the greatest cricketer Yorkshire ever produced, but easily the most elegantly dressed!'

At the A.G.M. in 1921, Bates was one of the three professionals hired at the pricely sum of £14 for every away match and £10 for each home game.

Eddie Bates did much fine work as a batsman for Glamorgan in their first eleven years as a first-class county, for he was a consistent batsman with a variety of strokes and a watchful defence.

He exceeded 1,000 runs in a season on seven occasions and scored ten centuries, with the best being an unbeaten 200 against Worcestershire at Kidderminster in 1927.

Possessing all the fighting qualities of a Yorkshireman, he was the only Glamorgan batsman to have a good season in 1925, scoring 919 runs. By 1926, Bates and Bell had developed into a sound opening pair, both batsmen passing the 1,000 run mark. Bates scored an unbeaten hundred to steer his side to an eight-wicket win over Derbyshire at Chesterfield – it was the County's first win of the season, Bates reaching his century after two hours' hard-hitting.

In 1927, though now at the veteran stage, he produced the best batting of his long career, just when his county needed it most. He ended the season with 1,645 runs at 44.45.

The county got off to a fine start in their opening match against

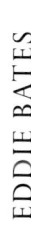

Essex at Leyton and were unlucky not to force a victory, the last Essex batsmen holding on for 35 minutes to gain a draw and still 180 runs short when time was called. The feature of the match was the batting of Bates, who scored a century in each innings, 105 and 111, to become the first Glamorgan player to achieve this feat. At Chesterfield, Glamorgan were lucky to escape with a draw, but had the worst of the wicket. The match was notable for the opening partnerships by N. V. H. Riches and Eddie Bates, the pair adding 148 in the first innings – the first instance of a three-figure opening partnership for the county – and 96 in the second innings. Later in the season, he hit his unbeaten double-hundred against Worcestershire, carrying his bat through an innings of 390.

The end of the 1927 season brought the sensation of the summer. Glamorgan travelled to Nottingham and were beaten by 122 runs, the return being played the following week at St Helen's. Nottinghamshire arrived at Swansea for what was the first match of the season, needing only to avoid defeat to win the Championship and that seemed a foregone conclusion as Glamorgan hadn't won a game. On a rain affected pitch, Nottinghamshire batted first and totalled 233. Bates and Bell opened with a partnership of 158 – Bates going on to make a vital contribution, scoring 163 in what was probably his best innings ever. His 'knock' included one six and 24 fours as Glamorgan scored 375 in reply – this against an attack consisting of Barratt, Staples, Richmond and Voce. After heavy rain, Notts tumbled to 61 all out, as Mercer (six for 31) and Ryan (four for 14) ripped through them, to give Glamorgan victory by an innings and 81 runs.

He had another good season in 1928, scoring 1,515 runs at an average of 33.66.

Towards the end of his playing days, he was greying and getting a little rotund, but he never lost his fighting spirit and made a good start to the 1930 season. Against Surrey at the Oval, Turnbull won the toss, and batting first, Glamorgan placed themselves reasonably safe from defeat by scoring 474 with Bates hitting 168. The rest of the match was notable for the fact that Jacks Hobbs scored a century in each innings of the match for the fifth time in his career.

The long service to the County by Eddie Bates was recognised in the visit of Yorkshire, being given to him as a benefit. It was most unfortunate for this fine player that rain interfered with the last two days' play, but it certainly saved his county from defeat. Glamorgan scored 262, with Bates getting a fifty, but Yorkshire could only muster 208 in reply. Then Verity took nine for 60, as the Welsh were dismissed for 113. Requiring 168 to win and with plenty of time, Yorkshire were 110 for 0 when rain ended the match!

By 1931, he was finding the spells of three-day cricket rather a strain and decided to retire. He had scored 12,802 runs and captured 239 wickets, with a best of eight for 93 v. Essex at Leyton in 1928, though normally the scoreboard was active while he was taking his turn with the ball.

He played a few matches for Cheshire in the Minor County Championship, before he went to live in Ireland, where he held several coaching engagements, and died in a Belfast hospital on 17th January 1957, at the age of 72.

JOSEPH BRAIN

Born: 11th September, 1863.
Kingswood, Bristol
Died: 26th June, 1914
Played: 1891-1908

GLAMORGAN RECORD

Innings	Not Out	Runs	H.Sc.	Average	100's
223	18	5283	144	25.77	4

Overs	Mdns	Runs	Wkts	Average	Best
88.4	14	275	19	14.47	6-60

NOTABLE FEATS
- He topped the Gloucestershire batting averages above W. G. Grace in 1884, after hitting 148 v. Surrey and 108 v. the Australian tourists.
- In 1896, he hit 144 for Glamorgan v. M.C.C. at Lord's.
- He was the Club's captain during their early days in the Minor County Championship.

Born at Kingswood, Bristol, Joseph Brain learned his cricket at Clifton College and Oxford University. He was in the Clifton XI in 1881-82-83, being captain in his last year and in the Oxford XI 1884 to 1887. As a Freshman, he was in the Varsity side which gained a memorable victory over the touring Australians.

He made his debut for Gloucestershire in 1883, and topped their averages the following season, above W. G. Grace, with scores that included 148 against Surrey and 108 against the Australians at Clifton. In 1885, he suffered a heart-breaking series of failures. For after scoring 135 against the M.C.C. at Lord's, his next six innings brought him three runs and four ducks! After playing for Gloucestershire in 1889, he returned to South Wales to become involved in the family's brewery business at Cardiff.

Brain was to become a dynamic force behind Glamorgan around the turn of the century, using his contacts in both the business and sporting worlds. He made great efforts to introduce talented Welsh youngsters, as well as being instrumental in getting several West Country amateurs to turn out for the Welsh county.

Following his move to Glamorgan, he added solidity to the Welsh side's middle order and became one of their most consistent batsmen in the Minor County Championship.

A match at the Arms Park had been arranged for publicity purposes by Brain, who became captain-secretary in 1892, though it cannot be said that he ever took quite the place that at one time seemed in store for him.

In 1896, he hit 144 for Glamorgan against the M.C.C. at Lord's and 170 in an hour-and-a-half for Cardiff against Clifton in 1899. Though there were defeats in 1896 at the hands of Surrey II and Worcestershire Club and Ground, he was able to take great satisfaction from the way his side had played that season.

He had a very strong belief that Glamorgan would only improve if they were to play in a higher standard of cricket and, preferably, on a league basis. Brain believed that the time was now right for his side to enter the recently formed Minor County Championship and after the M.C.C. had endorsed the Club's application, everyone looked forward to the 1897 season.

The Club ended the summer in second place and continued their improvement the following year, when their victories included a four-wicket win over a strong M.C.C. team.

Joseph Brain had few worries on the field of play, but this wasn't the case with the Club's finances. He had hoped to play the South African tourists in 1900, but an overdraft prevented the fixture from going ahead. However, he used his Varsity contacts and arranged a one-day game at the Arms Park in an effort to boost the club funds. Brain was able to give the townspeople of Cardiff the opportunity of watching some of the game's famous names in action at the Arms Park. For example, in 1900, W. D. Brownlee's XI, including Gilbert Jessop and Sammy Woods, met an XI captained by J. H. Brain. In 1900, the side ended the season on top of the table with Durham and Northamptonshire. Glamorgan's victories over Surrey II were the most praiseworthy – Brain made 102 out of 369 at the Arms Park and 88 out of 388 at the Oval, leading by example. Though the batting generally was not as strong as in the previous season, Brain finished top of the batting averages.

In 1902, Glamorgan's worries over finances were further eased when Brain secured a fixture against the Australian tourists at Cardiff, and though the match ended in a five-wicket win for the tourists, gate receipts exceeded £1,300. Within a couple of seasons, Joseph Brain was able to select a full strength Glamorgan XI, though he himself was laid low by an injury. In the previous season, Brain thought he had put his best side out for a game against the M.C.C., but unfortunately, Glamorgan were dismissed for 61 and 70 and lost by 108 runs on the final day. Brain was upset that his side were brushed aside as easily as they were, but his disappointment was eased when the visitors agreed to play an exhibition innings for the rest of the day to entertain the large crowd. Brain had a very good season behind the stumps in 1906, taking 24 catches and 17 stumpings, but at the end of the season, he decided to resign from the captaincy.

The 1908 season was Joseph Brain's final one as a player, though he remained on the Glamorgan committee to give support to 'Tal' Whittington, who shared Brain's desire to see the County go first-class.

From 1910, his health sadly declined and he died four years later after a heart-attack.

The *Western Mail* summed up his great contribution both on and off the field by saying that: 'his prowess at the wicket won him celebrity; his sportsmanship won him friendship; his generous patronage of the game won him gratitude'.

ALAN BUTCHER

Born: 7th January, 1954. Croydon
Played: 1987-1992

FIRST-CLASS GLAMORGAN RECORD

Innings	Not Out	Runs	H.Sc.	Average	100's
180	16	7324	171*	44.65	16

Overs	Mdns	Runs	Wkts	Average	Best
136.4	19	555	13	42.69	3-35

NOTABLE FEATS
- He scored 1,000 runs in a season for Glamorgan on 5 occasions, with a best of 2,116 in 1990.
- He hit 171* v. Warwickshire at Edgbaston in 1989.
- He hit 129 and 104 v. Lancashire at Liverpool in 1991.

GLAMORGAN'S seasoned opener, Alan Butcher played the best cricket of his life following his move from Surrey.

Yet, inconsistency was a word that came easily to mind when assessing his career at the Oval, though that inconsistency applied not only to Butcher, but to his treatment by the England selectors.

He began his career as a medium-pacer who could bat usefully, but soon found that opening was his forte. In the field, he remained a safe catcher, but his bowling declined to the extent where his looping spinners were used to encourage the opposition to declare! As a batsman, he was determined to go for his shots and was soon being talked of as an England player.

Despite some near misses, it was 1979 before Butcher scored 1,000 first-class runs in a season for the first time. International recognition soon followed when he was selected for the final Test against India at the Oval, but disappointingly, nerves got the better of him and scores of 14 and 20 were not enough to win him a tour place.

In 1980, he hit a century before lunch in the match against Glamorgan at the Oval and five years later, began his benefit year with the first Britannic Assurance Championship hundred of the season – again Glamorgan were the opponents!

He proved an able and popular deputy to both Roger Knight and Geoff Howarth, but in his benefit season, he was surprisingly relieved of the vice-captaincy. 'I'd like to captain a side, but not necessarily Surrey, I don't know why they stripped me of the vice-captaincy, but vice-captain is only really half a job with a manager, coach and captain.'

Little did he think that four years later his wish would come true. After falling out with the Surrey manager he left the Oval to join Glamorgan for the start of the 1987 season. During his 15 seasons with Surrey, he scored, 14,571 runs at 33.41 and captured 125 wickets at 37.51.

A courageous, left-handed batsman, and a particularly good player off the back foot, he has an attractive repertoire of strokes.

After badly damaging a calf muscle in the second month of the 1987 season, he returned to give an illustration of his best form by scoring centuries against Leicestershire, Worcestershire and Derbyshire.

In the match against Derbyshire, he had to retire midway

through his innings after being hit on the arm, but returned to face the hostile Derbyshire attack and protect the lower order. His score stayed on 99 for several overs as he refused a number of singles so that last man Steve Barwick would not have to face Michael Holding. Butcher eventually got his century and ended the summer with 1,007 runs and was awarded his County cap.

The following summer, he hit 166 against Cambridge University, who had been the opposition when he hit his highest score for Surrey, 216 not out in 1980.

Alan Butcher might have been thought to be heading towards retirement when, in 1989, Hugh Morris stepped down from the captaincy and it passed to his opening partner. That the responsibility suited him can be gauged from the fact that in all matches he made 1,632 runs, a supply which showed no signs of drying up.

An example of Butcher's tactical skill as a captain came in the 1990 match against India at St Helen's when, after Azharuddin had played a couple of wristy leg-glances, he moved Matthew Maynard across to leg-slip and within four balls, India's captain was caught in the trap. It was a summer when Butcher returned a career-best aggregate in all matches of 2,116 runs. He hit a magnificent 104 in the Nat West quarter-final at Lord's, which several judges considered to be one of the finest innings seen in limited-overs cricket all season.

He was also the first Englishman to pass 1,000 runs and was beaten only by those phenomenal openers, Jimmy Cook and Desmond Haynes.

In 1991, I witnessed at first hand the tremendous batting form of Alan Butcher since he joined Glamorgan. Not a season had gone by without the man from Croydon making 1,000 runs and against Lancashire at Liverpool in late June, he made 129 and 104 in fine style. In fact, if he had been a little younger, everyone would have been putting his name forward for the Test side again – perhaps it is worth making the point that Graham Gooch is seven months older!

Alan Butcher has enjoyed his cricket and proved himself among the shrewdest captains on the circuit and the most successful Glamorgan have had since their County Championship winning days in 1969. Now captain and coach of the Essex 2nd XI, Alan's son Gary made his Glamorgan debut in 1994.

– Famous Cricketers of Glamorgan –

JOHNNY CLAY

Born: 18th March, 1898. Bonvilston
Died: 11th August, 1973
Played: 1921-1949

FIRST-CLASS GLAMORGAN RECORD

Innings	Not Out	Runs	H.Sc.	Average	100's
536	88	6868	155*	15.33	2

Overs	Mdns	Runs	Wkts	Average	Best
9911.1	2326	25181	1292	19.49	9-54

NOTABLE FEATS

- He shares the Glamorgan 9th wickets record partnerships of 203* with J. J. Hills v. Worcestershire at Swansea in 1929.
- In 1935, he took nine for 54 v. Northamptonshire at Llanelli and topped the national averages with 56 wickets at 12.73.
- In 1936, he took eight for 14 in 66 balls v. India at Swansea.
- He took nine for 59 v. Essex at Westcliff in 1937, a season in which he also took nine for 66 v. Worcestershire at Swansea to return match figures of 17 for 211.
- He has taken 100 wickets in a season for Glamorgan on three occasions.
- He holds the Glamorgan record for the highest number of first-class wickets in a season – 176 at 17.34 in 1937.
- In 1946, he took 130 wickets at 12.40.

O<small>NE OF CRICKET</small>'<small>S</small> most interesting personalities, Johnny Clay was a product of Winchester School, where he was regarded as an all-rounder; he played in the XI under first Gilbert and then Hubert Ashton, generally as a pace bowler, though in 1915, he beat Wellington, more or less single-handed, when he took nine wickets for 43 with leg-breaks.

In his early playing days, Johnny Clay was a fast bowler of genuine merit. In fact, J. H. Morgan in his book 'Glamorgan' had no doubt that Clay was the fastest of all time for the Welsh side.

Johnny Clay (left) with Norman Riches and Trevor Arnott.

He made his debut for Glamorgan in 1921, after having played against them for Monmouthshire the previous season. In 1922, he bowled leg-cutters at a brisk pace, besides the occasional experiments with leg-spin to end the season as the side's leading wicket-taker with 83 wickets at an average of 22.01. Clay replaced Whittington as captain in 1924, leading the team through a very important period of their history, in 1926 taking top place in the County Championship early in the season, the only time that Glamorgan had led the way until 1948. The claims of business compelled Clay to resign the captaincy at the end of the 1927 season.

It was a season when he amazed his friends and amused himself by scoring a century against the touring New Zealanders. Glamorgan wanted 406 to win in four and a half hours but Clay going in at No. 4, played his natural attacking game and completely dominated the scoring. Glamorgan lost six wickets for 69 runs, but Clay completed a hard-hitting hundred out of 149 in two-and-a-quarter hours – his unbeaten 115 was the highest score of his career.

Although obviously better known as a bowler, his batting was by no means indistinguished. He revelled in the fierce drive and could be excellent in a crisis. In the 354 matches he played for Glamorgan, he scored 6,868 runs and batted in almost every position from No. 1 to No. 11 and at one time, went in before Arnold Dyson and Emrys Davies, who were to become Glamorgan's most successful pair.

Johnny Clay will always hold an honoured place in the history of Glamorgan, not only for his ability as a cricketer, but also because of his high personal qualities.

He was a man of charming disposition, with a high sense of humour – who else would have bowled a rubber ball in a first-class county match – and get away with it! The match was against Somerset at Weston – C. C. Case was batting, when Clay hurled down the red rubber ball with the speed of one of his old time quickies. It pitched on a good length and bounced over the batsman's and wicket-keeper's heads until it reached the boundary – play was held up to give players and umpires time to regain normality.

In 1933 in the match against Leicestershire at Cardiff, he shook the cricket world by reverting to under-hand bowling. Leicestershire were piling up a big score and Shipman had got a hundred before a good length ball with plenty of finger spin turned quickly and he was bowled – by a lob. How the crowd roared! Later in the season, he had the temerity to bowl the big-hitting Arthur Wellard of Somerset with a similar delivery.

For many years, he always carried a tennis-ball in his right-hand jacket pocket where he constantly pressed and twisted it to keep his fingers flexible. He did not simply spin the ball; he also had the gift of the natural finger spinner to make it dip or to bounce high, often faster than the batsman guessed.

Errol Holmes has described how, in his first Championship match as captain of Surrey in 1934, Clay found an Oval pitch to help him and bowled Surrey out twice in a day, Hobbs and Sandham and all. Clay bowled unchanged from the pavilion end for five hours and took 12 wickets for 84. Glamorgan won by an innings and 92 runs, and they had never won a match at the Oval before. Holmes considered Clay 'as good as any off-spinner I have ever seen'.

In the match against Northamptonshire at Llanelli in 1935, the visitors batted first and made a good start, but Clay attacked the tail with such venom that he took the last eight wickets in 14.2 overs, his final analysis being nine for 54 in the innings of 137. Glamorgan followed and scored 158 for four by the end of the day. Clay bowled well again when Northamptonshire batted a second time, his six for 32 including six of the first seven batsmen as Glamorgan won by an innings and 109 runs. He was the side's leading bowler that season with 65 wickets in all matches at 13.30 runs each. His bowling performances that summer were brought to the attention of the Test selectors and he was 12th man for the Tests at Headingley and Old Trafford. If Johnny Clay had not positively shrugged off the selectors and insisted that he was not available for overseas tours, he must have played often for England.

In the event, he did so only once at the Oval in that series against South Africa – when his sense of the rightness of things was disturbed by the fact that his cricket bag was sent to Lord's in error and he had to take the field in someone else's ill-fitting clothes!

The following season the August Bank Holiday match with the Indian touring team was affected by rain but India, batting for a second time, needed 126 runs to avoid an innings defeat. Clay was bowling with deadly effect and the ninth wicket fell at 49 with his figures then reading eight for 14, but the last wicket added 65 very quick runs, 29 of them off Clay in three overs – very heavy punishment for that most accurate of bowlers.

He headed the Glamorgan bowling averages in eleven seasons, with his greatest year being 1937, when he captured a record 176 wickets at 17.34 runs each. Against Worcestershire at Swansea, he took nine for 66 and eight for 146 to create a new Glamorgan record. In the next match, Yorkshire were reduced to 50 for six as Clay dismissed Hutton, Sutcliffe, Barber and Mitchell, but later rallied to 255. The rains came and ended any thoughts Clay may have had about regaining his Test place. He also took 14 wickets against Essex at Westcliff and 13 in the return game at Llanelli – it was the first time they had beaten Essex in sixteen years and within a couple of weeks, Glamorgan had accomplished the double. Johnny Clay was the driving force behind the County's wartime fixtures and in 1944, took seven for 43 as the Army were beaten at Newport. Following Turnbull's tragic death, the Club was left without a captain, but Clay was unanimously elected for 1946.

His side surpassed all expectations, finishing sixth. Clay's captaincy was the linchpin of the team's success. He was not afraid to make interesting challenges and cleverly handled his bowling attack. He was a great crowd-pleaser – the match between Glamorgan and the Indian touring team at Cardiff that season was constantly interrupted by rain. So, when soon after tea on Bank Holiday, the Glamorgan innings was ended by Sarwate bowling Peter Judge, Clay thought the spectators ought not to be frustrated by another stoppage. So as captain and the not out batsman, he turned to Vijay Merchant and said: 'Shall we follow-on right away to save boring the crowd?' Merchant agreed and Sarwate clean bowled Judge again for what must certainly have been the fastest 'pair of spectacles' – about half a minute – in the history of any form of cricket. At this ripe age of 48, he ended the season with 130 wickets at 12.40 apiece.

Yet, during the winter months, he felt that his playing days were drawing to a close and announced his resignation as captain and semi-retirement from county cricket saying that 'to be captain of a county side is a full-time job and I have many interests and other things to do. There is less need for me to carry on when we have a fully qualified captain in Mr Wooller ready at hand.'

Though he only played in 13 games in 1947, he still managed to take 54 wickets in the Championship at 15.83. His best game was at the Arms Park when he took six for 5 against Leicestershire in an 11-over spell.

During the 1948 Championship winning season, Clay had match figures of ten for 65 as Glamorgan beat Surrey by an innings and 24 runs. Retained for the next match against Hampshire at Bournemouth, he had match figures of nine for 79, including six for 48 in the second innings as the Welsh side won by an innings and 115 runs to win the title. Clay summed up his feelings of delight by saying: 'It is the greatest thing that has ever happened in my life to see Glamorgan win the Championship.'

Called 'the father of Glamorgan cricket', he certainly did his best to keep the family happy. The triumph of 1948, when he was 50 years of age, was one of the most satisfying of cricket endings.

PHIL CLIFT

Born: 3rd September, 1918. Usk
Played: 1937-1955

FIRST-CLASS GLAMORGAN RECORD

Innings	Not Out	Runs
306	21	6055
H.Sc.	Average	100's
125*	21.24	7

Overs	Mdns	Runs	Wkts	Average	Best
216.2	38	675	11	61.36	3-6

NOTABLE FEATS
- He scored 1,000 runs in a season for Glamorgan on 3 occasions.

PHIL CLIFT who was to give yeoman service to the Club on and off the field, joined the staff in 1936 and made his first-class debut the following season, following a series of fine innings for Glamorgan Colts – he was just 16 years of age.

In 1947, Glamorgan travelled to Trent Bridge and batting first on a batsman's paradise, were all out for 234. On the second day, Nottinghamshire declared at 384 for five, but on the last day, Glamorgan batted steadily to make 360 for four – Phil Croft scoring his maiden century, an unbeaten 100, though the match ended in a draw.

However, he did not gain a regular place in the County side until 1948, when he replaced Arnold Dyson as Emrys Davies's opening partner and gained his County cap.

Clift was an attractive stylist with many punishing shots in his repertoire. While Davies took his time, Clift liked to hit the ball hard if it was well pitched up to him. Occasionally, he was in difficulty to a late swinging delivery with the new ball, but at other times, he upset the opposition attack with some very quick run-scoring.

So impressed was Don Bradman in 1948, that he described Clift as one of the best prospects in the country. Clift was also an excellent fielder close to the bat and was a vital member of the leg trap which steered Glamorgan to their first Championship that season, as he held 26 catches, including six in the match against Sussex at Swansea.

In 1949, he passed 1,000 runs for the season for the first time. His top score was 125 not out against Derbyshire at Cardiff, though one of his most remarkable innings that summer came against Essex at Ebbw Vale.

The Essex captain Tom Pearce declared setting Glamorgan 177 to win in 105 minutes. Phil Croft responded to Pearce's challenge with an unbeaten 101, hitting the England all-rounder Trevor Bailey for six in his opening over. In fact, Clift added a further fourteen boundaries in his 79 minute occupancy of the crease, as Glamorgan reached the target in 24 overs and for the loss of only one wicket!

During the 1949-50 winter, he coached in South Africa, but was taken ill on the way home and missed the whole of the 1950 season completely. Clift's career was dogged by bouts of illness and an operation in the 1950s took the edge from his batting. He played his last game for the Welsh County in 1955 and decided to retire, taking over the duties of coaching organiser with Brian Edrich as his assistant. During the winter months he tirelessly ran the indoor schools at Cardiff and Neath and organised and captained the Second Eleven and Colts teams. In fact, almost every young Glamorgan cricketer between the 1950s and 1970s came under his wing, as he established himself as one of the best coaches in the country.

The County coach when Glamorgan won the Championship in 1969, he was proud that six young men he selected and developed were members of that side. Shy and retiring, he got the best out of the youngsters, because they trusted and respected him, and he, too, was a member of the 1948 side.

Phil also assisted his friend Wilf Wooller with the administration of the Club, and was appointed Assistant Secretary in 1972. It was inevitable that Phil would eventually succeed Wooller as Secretary and in 1977, he was appointed as the Club's new Secretary.

There were several changes in the Club at the end of the 1982 season, and one of these saw Phil Clift announce his retirement after over forty years with Glamorgan as player, coach and administrator – he was richly rewarded with a Testimonial in recognition of his service. He has maintained his links with the Club after his retirement, by scoring for both the first and second teams, besides helping to manage the Glamorgan Under-19 team.

TONY CORDLE

Born: 21st September, 1940.
Bridgewater, Barbados
Played: 1963-1980

FIRST-CLASS GLAMORGAN RECORD

Innings	Not Out	Runs
433	76	5239
H.Sc.	Average	100's
81	14.67	–

Overs	Mdns	Runs	Wkts	Average	Best
7013.5	1615	19281	701	27.50	9-49

NOTABLE FEATS
- He took nine for 49 v. Leicestershire at Colwyn Bay in 1969.
- He performed the hat-trick v. Hampshire at Portsmouth in a John Player League game in 1979.

A NTHONY ELTON CORDLE was born on 21st September 1940, the son of a writ server and court officer at St Michael, one of the eleven parishes into which the island of Barbados is divided. At the age of 22, he had a most unusual occupation, mixing the flavours in a mineral water factory. Tony's brother Steve was a seaman, but had to give up the sea after losing an eye in an accident. He came to Britain, where he got a job in Cardiff. Then Tony's sister Joan went to Cardiff to continue her studies in midwifery and nursing.

Britain beckoned for Tony and he followed his brother and sister in January 1961. Making his way to London, he got his first job, as station man on the Underground. After just ten days with London Transport, he wrote to his relatives in Cardiff and asked if there was any chance of a home and work in Wales. His brother found him a room and very soon off went Tony to the Labour Exchange.

He landed a job as shunter with British Rail and while he was upstairs in the Labour Exchange waiting to be interviewed, he looked down into the old Cardiff Arms Park cricket ground. Tony's eyes took in the square and scoreboard and he felt a great drive to play there, yet, he had never heard of Glamorgan! He knew about Lancashire, Surrey and Yorkshire and Hampshire, but only because Roy Marshall played for them.

After starting work as a shunter, he walked over to the ground and said that he would like to join the club – it was explained to him that this was a professional organisation competing at national level! He was then asked if he played any club cricket back home in Barbados – Tony's reply was priceless: 'No, but I've played with a bat and ball on Sunday mornings.' Tony Cordle had one thing to commend him – a strong physique – but Glamorgan noted he had speed as well as strength after he'd spent a few moments in the indoor nets. He just picked up the ball and knowing nothing about seam up or how to hold the ball, ran to the wicket and let it go!

The County decided to play him in a club game in April 1962 on a Sunday, when he was free from his shunting duties. It was the first time that he had played in boots – bowling his first delivery off the wrong foot, he sent the middle stump flying. He finished with five for 18 and one of the most improbable of all first-class careers was about to take shape.

He made his first-class debut in a friendly with Cambridge University at Margam in the shadow of the Welsh steel works in 1963. Another year and Cordle found himself out of the shunting yard for half a year with a professional contract in his pocket. He continued to make steady improvement and formed a useful opening partnership with the new ball with Jeff Jones. By 1966, he had established himself as a first-team regular and the following year was able to wear the blue cap with the daffodil emblem on it.

Tony then had to spend a couple of winters on the dole before he got a job working in the University Hospital of Wales stores in Cardiff, but he was bowling so well that he knew he would never have to consider doing this job all the year round.

In 1969, the Colwyn Bay ground was allocated an annual fixture – the first being against Leicestershire. A demon on his day, he took nine for 49, which was the best individual bowling performance of the season in the championship – not bad when you consider that seven years earlier he had never even heard of thirteen teams in the championship!

After two disappointing summers the Glamorgan committee decided that the time had come to make way for new talent and one of the players they decided to axe was Tony Cordle. Yet, by the time the 1972 season had ended, the County had wisely had second thoughts of getting rid of a man who could always prove himself useful, especially in the one-day game.

In 1979, he bravely shouldered the brunt of the bowling and finished up as leading wicket-taker with 58 victims. It was a season in which Hampshire felt the full force of the friendly Barbadian in the one-day competitions. He turned in his two best performances against the southern county in the Benson and Hedges Cup, taking four for 14 at Swansea, whilst in the John Player League, he took five for 24, including a hat-trick in the match at Portsmouth.

The following season, he played his last game for the County, finishing his first-class career with 701 wickets at 27.50.

A Barbadian with a big, infectious grin, his flashes of talent and power made Tony Cordle worth watching whatever the state of the game or the weather.

HARRY CREBER

Born: 30th April, 1872. Birkenhead
Died: 27th March, 1939
Played: 1898-1922

FIRST-CLASS GLAMORGAN RECORD

Innings	Not Out	Runs	H.Sc.	Average	100's
300	108	1779	52	9.27	0

Overs	Mdns	Runs	Wkts	Average	Best
7245.0	1776	19570	1225	15.98	9-91

NOTABLE FEATS
- In 1906, he took 103 wickets to break G. J. Thompson's tally in a season for a Minor County.

Glamorgan County Cricket Club, 1921-2. Harry Creber is on the far right of the back row. Also pictured is Jack Nash, second right, back row.

For most of the Minor County seasons, Harry Creber along with Jack Nash kept each end going – thus from the earliest days of the County, the phrase 'the brunt of the bowling fell on two players' came into use.

In 1899, the Swansea-based left-arm bowler took 13 wickets in the victory over Monmouthshire and 14 in both of the games against Berkshire. The following season saw Glamorgan finish top of the Championship table, sharing the honours of Champions with Durham and Northamptonshire. Creber was again the Club's most successful bowler, taking eight for 75 in the creditable draw with Northamptonshire at the Arms Park, but overall, his cost per wicket was higher than the previous season.

In the August Bank Holiday match at Cardiff in 1902, against the Australians, he took four wickets for 65 runs for a combined Glamorgan and Wiltshire side, and twice enjoyed the distinction of dismissing Clem Hill, the great left-handed batsman.

At the end of the 1904 season, the County finished in third place and had it not been laid low by injuries, it is likely that the Championship would have come home to South Wales. Creber took 76 wickets and Nash 66, and as usual sent down the majority of the overs, 849 of the 1,056 bowled.

In 1905, Creber often had to bowl unchanged throughout a match and through sheer perseverance, he was rewarded with a record

100 wickets to equal Thompson's tally in a season for a Minor County. Creber went even better the following summer, taking 103 wickets, though the side as a whole had a disappointing season. In 1908, he took eight for 18 as Glamorgan dismissed Wiltshire for 41 in the semi-final of the Minor County Championship, but the side lost to Staffordshire in the final.

The summer of 1913 saw Glamorgan make another bid for Championship honours, and at the end of the season, tied for first place with Norfolk. The eastern county was met in the Challenge match at Norwich in September, but the rain ruined the first two days' play, and Norfolk won the Championship by a first innings decision. Norfolk won the Championship by a first innings decision. Norfolk batted first and scored 173 for three on the first day and, on the second, lost their last seven wickets for 71 runs. In reply, Glamorgan scored 54 runs without loss, but on the last morning, the innings total only reached 168. With a lead of 76 runs, Norfolk fared badly at their second attempt, being dismissed for 61. Harry Creber's figures were:

O.	M.	R.	W.
12.4	1	38	8

but there was insufficient time available for Glamorgan to try and get the 138 runs needed for victory.

Persuaded to come out of retirement for 1921, Creber acted as the fourth professional for the side in their first season in first-class cricket. He was now 47 – a puckish figure, he could certainly be mischievous when in the mood. He believed in 'feeding' certain types of batsmen, but always when he was bowling, he was thinking out ways and means to lure the batsman to his fate.

As a batsman himself, he only reached double figures in four of the 58 first-class innings he played for Glamorgan – his first double-figure score coming in his 31st innings.

In 1921 and 1922, he took 95 wickets (45 at 27.62 and 50 at 26.14) before retiring to become head groundsman and cricket professional at Swansea and so retain his association with Glamorgan cricket.

Harry Creber died on 27th March 1939 at the age of 65, yet no matter what the weather, he would always be found tending to his beloved turf – never in a jacket, always in his Welsh flannelette shirt!

DAI DAVIES

Born: 26th August, 1896. Llanelli
Died: 16th July, 1976
Played: 1923-1939

FIRST-CLASS GLAMORGAN RECORD

Innings	Not Out	Runs
681	61	15008
H.Sc.	Average	100's
216	24.20	16

Overs	Mdns	Runs	Wkts	Average	Best
3661.4	774	9404	271	34.70	6-50

NOTABLE FEATS

- In 1923, he carried his bat through a completed innings, scoring 100* out of 161 v. Worcestershire at Worcester.
- He shares the Glamorgan 8th wicket partnership record of 202 v. Sussex at Eastbourne in 1928 with J. J. Hills.
- In 1928, he scored three centuries in successive innings in first-class matches; 126* v. Sussex at Swansea, 103 v. Northants at Northampton and 165* v. Sussex at Eastbourne.
- He scored 1,000 runs in a season for Glamorgan on seven occasions.
- He scored 216 v. Somerset at Newport in 1939.

DAI DAVIES held a very special place in the hearts of Glamorgan supporters. Not only was he for many years an indispensable member of the County side, but he and his namesake, Emrys, who was no relation, were the first home-born professionals to find regular places in it.

Dai was never one of the game's acknowledged stylists, but with a keen eye and good timing, remained with the County for sixteen years, scoring 15,008 runs at the end of the them, besides taking 271 wickets and holding 194 catches. Yet more importantly than his material contribution was that he was one of the first to prove that the Welsh temperament could adjust from Rugby football to the subtleties of first-class cricket.

Dai Davies's entry into first-class cricket is perhaps one of the most romantic stories the game has ever recorded.

After five matches of the 1923 season, Glamorgan were still waiting for their first success. It was almost in desperation that the Committee decided to bring in Dai for the match against Northamptonshire at Swansea. It was a brave decision, for Dai was unknown outside of his own Llanelli. At the time, he was a just a solid, conscientious club cricketer and uncoached in the finer points of the game. His first game was typical of his career. He had been working a long night shift at the local steel works and was fast asleep in bed about 10 o'clock in the morning, when his well-earned rest was disturbed by his mother who explained to the startled Dai, 'There's a car at the door for you; they want you to play in a cricket match or something.'

The Club had sent a car for Dai on the very first morning of the match against Northamptonshire – the game being due to start within an hour or two and Swansea was twelve miles away!

After snatching a spot of breakfast he was soon racing to Swansea, but the game was already in progress when he arrived at the ground. However, the gateman would not believe Dai that he was wanted to play. There was a slight delay before the Glamorgan secretary Arthur Gibson arrived to put things right. Eventually he got onto the field, but Northants were then 40 for 0. When he was put on to bowl, he took a wicket in his fourth over, and two more before lunch for just ten runs. He came in to bat on the second day, when Glamorgan were 131 for 7 and played magnificently to score 58 runs, being last man out at 253. He opened the batting in the second innings and scored 51, and Glamorgan won a rare victory.

Until it was equalled by Gilbert Parkhouse, he held the Glamorgan record of scoring three centuries in successive innings. That was in 1928 when in three consecutive 'knocks' he scored 126* v. Sussex at Swansea, 103 v. Northants at Northampton and 165* v. Sussex at Eastbourne. In his next match against Gloucestershire at Pontypridd, Charlie Parker dismissed him for 0 in each innings! He ended the season with 1,213 runs at an average of 32.78 and was rewarded with selection at the end of the season for the Players in their annual match with the Gentlemen, scoring 54 before rain put an end to his innings.

Dai was a typical Welshman and when batting was happiest if he had a partner with whom he could call the runs in Welsh. This not only confused the opposition in moments of normality, but even more so in moments of crisis, because Dai would run up the wicket for a quick single shouting in Welsh 'No go back!'

A solid and determined batsman, he had plenty of scoring strokes, especially in front of the wicket. He was also a useful medium-paced off-spinner and a superb cover fielder.

In 1939, Glamorgan were involved in a high-scoring draw against Somerset. The Welsh crowd were quite rightly enraged with their opponents' slow play, for it took them until almost lunch on the second day to make 385. Turnbull was also incensed and told his opposite number that he would keep them in the field for the rest of the match. Glamorgan amassed 574 for seven – Dai Davies taking the opportunity to show sympathy with the striking Monmouthshire miners at the nearby Bedwas Colliery. He had asked Emrys Davies to let him know when the strike finished. Emrys waved to him at around six o'clock that the miners protest was over, so after nearly nine hours at the crease, Dai immediately went down the wicket and was stumped for a career best score of 216!

Dai announced his retirement at the end of the 1939 season, intimating that he wanted to be an umpire.

So when he reappeared in 1946, it was as an umpire. He remained on the first-class list until 1961 and during that time, he umpired in 23 Tests. As might be expected, he was firm and decisive and was as much respected in this second part of his career as he had been in the first.

Perhaps his most famous moment came in 1948, when he was umpiring Glamorgan v. Hampshire at Bournemouth. Hampshire's last man, Charlie Knott was hit on the pads in front of the wicket and all the close fielders made a rousing appeal to which Dai said: 'That's out and we've won the Championship!'

In August 1951, he dismissed the immortal Len Hutton for 'obstructing the field' when South African wicket-keeper Russell Endean scrambled around him to make a catch which Hutton flicked out of his way. Umpiring his last match in 1961, he remained a devout and respected man, and would have carried on much longer had he not been severely handicapped with arthritis.

His sudden death, one month short of his eightieth birthday, marked the end of one of the great characters who served Glamorgan cricket in the years when the Welsh County was finding its first-class feet.

EMRYS DAVIES

Born: 27th June, 1904. Llanelli
Died: 10th November, 1975
Played: 1924-1954

FIRST-CLASS GLAMORGAN RECORD

Innings	Not Out	Runs	H.Sc.	Average	100's
1016	79	26102	287*	27.85	31

Overs	Mdns	Runs	Wkts	Average	Best
10263.4	2359	26030	885	29.41	6-24

NOTABLE FEATS

- He did the 'double' on two occasions for Glamorgan in 1935 and 1937.
- He carried his bat through an innings on two occasion, with 155* out of 340 v. Somerset at Weston-super-Mare in 1935 the best.
- He performed the hat-trick v. Leicestershire at Leicester in 1937, also hitting 139.
- His best season with the bat was 1937 when he scored 1,954 runs at 39.87.
- He scored 287* v. Gloucestershire at Newport in 1939.
- He took 24 runs off an over from G. V. Gunn of Nottinghamshire at Swansea in 1939.
- He scored 215 v. Essex at Brentwood in 1948.
- He scored 1,000 runs in a season for Glamorgan on 16 occasions.
- He shares the Glamorgan third-wicket record partnership of 313 with W. E. Jones v. Essex at Brentwood in 1948.

EMRYS DAVIES was not a natural cricket genius. He reached the top only by hard work and his progress was quite slow. In fact, after a few years on the staff, there were some Committee members who wanted to dispense with his services, for he couldn't command a regular place in the side. Indeed, but for the judgement and insistence that he stay by Johnny Clay, the County would have let him go.

Emrys Davies coaching.

He first appeared in 1924, but despite plenty of opportunities, it wasn't until 1932 that he made his place secure by scoring over 1,000 runs, which he continued to do every year until 1953 (though he played a few matches to help out in 1954). This was also the year that he started his long association with Arnold Dyson as the County's opening batsmen. They were soon to be recognised as one of the most formidable and consistent pairs in English cricket. They took part in 32 century partnerships during the ten seasons they opened the innings – a record which would have been easily excelled had it not been for the intervention of war at a time when they were both at their peak.

In the last match of the 1935 season, Emrys Davies dismissed Worcestershire's Frank Warne on the final afternoon to become the first Glamorgan player to achieve the 'double' – he made 1,326 runs (at 28.21) and took 100 wickets (at 21.07).

The summer of 1937 was a memorable one for him. He achieved the 'double' again scoring 2,012 runs in all matches and capturing 103 wickets. It was a rare performance, not sufficiently noticed, since it was overshadowed by the extraordinary performance that same season of Jim Parks, who took 100 wickets and scored three thousand runs! Davies shared in a record opening partnership of 274 with Arnold Dyson that season at Leicester and then took a hat-trick as Glamorgan won by an innings at Leicester and then took a hat-trick as Glamorgan won by an innings and 49 runs. He excelled in many games that summer, perhaps none more so than in the second game of the season against the New Zealand tourists. In their first innings, Glamorgan totalled 229, with Davies hitting a steady half-century, before New Zealand struggled to an overnight score of 116 for seven. The following morning, Emrys took the remaining three wickets for one run as Glamorgan gained a 102 run lead. This was extended further, with Davies hitting 78, as the tourists were set 443 to win. Emrys took a further three wickets in the final session as Glamorgan went on to win by 322 runs.

Emrys batted and bowled left-handed. He was essentially a sound and imperturbable batsman and a good player of fast bowling. He was also quick on his feet and a fine driver of the ball, both straight and to the off, whilst he was by no means deficient in shots to the leg-side. As a bowler, he flighted the ball skilfully and was never afraid to toss it up. Emrys, though, lacked the vicious spin that makes his type of bowling a dread when the ball is turning; he was primarily a hard wicket bowler. A good fieldsman, he had a remarkably safe pair of hands and it was quite an event when he dropped a catch.

Against Gloucestershire at Newport in 1939, he scored a record 287 not out as Glamorgan needed 309 to avoid an innings defeat. Hammond had scored a majestic 302 and Davies might have even surpassed his score, but the Gloucestershire captain stationed all his fielders on the boundary edge during the final stages of the game.

At the end of that season, Glamorgan supporters were cheered by the news that Davies had been selected for the England tour of India, but war was declared soon after and the tour was cancelled.

During the 1939-45 war, Emrys enlisted in the Army. In 1946, he was posted to Cardiff barracks and was allowed to join the Glamorgan side. Though he wasn't demobbed until late July, he managed to play in all the Championship games by doing guard duty all night so that he could play during the day in home matches and 'obtaining' privilege leave to coincide with away games.

In 1947, the return match with Sussex at Cardiff was won by four wickets and it is memorable for the two century opening partnerships by Arnold Dyson and Emrys Davies. Glamorgan put themselves out of danger by a good innings on the opening day and very consistent bowling forced Sussex to follow-on. A recovery enabled Sussex to set Glamorgan 151 runs to win. Dyson and Davies took the score to 116 before they were parted, but six wickets fell before Glamorgan scored the winning run. The side then travelled to Southampton and for the third innings in succession a century opening partnership by Dyson and Emrys Davies was recorded, this being the main factor in the County's ten wicket win.

It was after the war that Emrys became affectionately known by his team-mates as 'The Rock', the solid base on which the new Glamorgan arose. In 1948 he was the leading run-getter with 1,708 runs at an average of 36.34, when Glamorgan won the Championship for the first time. It was a fact that after so many years spent struggling at the other end of the table he steadfastly refused to believe it until he heard it on the wireless!

In 1952 at the age of 48, Emrys produced some magical performances to finish the season as leading run-scorer with over 1,700 runs, yet without a century. He was also one of the side's fittest and nimblest fielders, showing no signs of age.

The summer of 1954 saw the retirement of Emrys Davies. It came suddenly at Peterborough where Frank Tyson bowled the 50-year-old Glamorgan stalwart with a scorching delivery. On returning to the pavilion he took off his cap and gloves, unfastened his pads and then with tears in his eyes told Wilf Wooller: 'Skipper, I am finished. I can no longer see the ball.'

True to his word, he never batted again for the Club and at the end of the season became a first-class umpire.

One of the most popular players ever to play for Glamorgan, he could not have given thirty years loyal service to the Club and sustained such a wonderful record without exceptional qualities – he scored 26,102 runs – an aggregate only exceeded by Alan Jones – took 885 wickets and held 221 catches – Glamorgan owe him a big debt.

As an umpire, he was good enough to stand in two Tests, but he had not the health for those long, patient hours standing still. He was, however, a successful coach at Llandovery College and also in South Africa.

Emrys was a man universally loved and respected, especially by the young players, whom he went out of his way to help and put at ease. He even found it in his heart to offer words of advice and encouragement to the up and coming Fred Trueman on one of those days when Fred's youthful pace and fire were being dampened by a loss of rhythm and accuracy.

An esteemed man and longest-serving Glamorgan professional, he died at his home in Llanelli, aged 71, after a protracted illness.

HAYDN DAVIES

Born: 23rd April, 1912. Llanelli
Died: 4th September, 1993
Played: 1935-1958

FIRST-CLASS GLAMORGAN RECORD

Innings	Not Out	Runs
596	95	6515
H.Sc.	Average	100's
80	13.00	–

Overs	Mdns	Runs	Wkts	Average	Best
3.0	0	20	1	20.00	1-20

NOTABLE FEATS
- He made 782 dismissals (580 caught, 202 stumped) in his career with Glamorgan.
- In 1939, he helped to dismiss six Leicestershire batsmen in an innings in the match at Leicester.
- In 1955, he helped to dismiss eight South African batsmen in the match at Swansea.
- His best season behind the stumps was 1955 when he helped to dismiss 82 batsmen.
- He holds the Glamorgan record for playing in the highest first-class total without conceding a bye – 422 for 8 dec v. Gloucestershire at Swansea in 1957.

Haydn Davies was one of the few players of his day in first-class cricket to persuade the paying public that character and the day of 'characters' in cricket had not ended. Because he thought much of, and much about, the game, with considerable ability, he was bound to make an impression on the cricket of his time.

He became a member of the Glamorgan staff in 1935, almost fresh from the University of Wales. Although he didn't get a regular place immediately, he showed that he had the ability to press for a first-team place and after a promising debut, he was offered a contract for the following season. Yet, it was 1938, when he took over the gloves from T. L. Brierley on a regular basis, and once he had made the spot his own, he was never displaced.

While his hitting won matches for Glamorgan, his defence showed in other matches against the odds. In the 1939 Bank Holiday match against the West Indies, which ended inside two days with a two wicket victory for the tourists, Davies was prominent. Wickets fell fast on the first day, but the second day's play was full of interest, with Haydn Davies and E. C. Jones adding 80 for the eighth wicket when a heavy defeat seemed likely. During the match, Davies dismissed seven batsmen, all caught, whilst in the match against Leicestershire, he dismissed six batsmen in an innings. He ended the season with 69 victims – 50 caught and 19 stumped. During the war he served in the Army, being a captain in the Royal Artillery.

Though the war robbed him of years which were vital to his development, it didn't take him too long to reach the top as a wicket-keeper. Haydn Davies's wicket-keeping was recognised during the season of 1946 when he was selected to play for The Rest v. England in the Test trial at Lord's. He was very unlucky not to go to Australia at the end of the season, but the selectors demanded more than of others who were chosen. Also, it was the advent of Kent's Godfrey Evans that spoilt any prospect he had of Test honours. Yet, as all Welsh cricket followers will know, Haydn Davies stood high enough in his own branch of the game not to have been out of place in a Test match.

However, there were some spectators who were decided into thinking that because of his heavy build and shambling movement behind the stumps, he was slow – but, in fact, that shamble helped maintain perfect balance at far greater speed than that of some of his more acrobatic contemporaries. He was without doubt, one of the best wicket-keepers of his day; no keeper in the country was better on the leg-side. He took some miraculous catches and stumpings and he too performed some acrobatic stops, all against the forces of equilibrium!

Haydn Davies always kept his eagerness until the end of the

longest day's play – playing his part to the full in the County Championship-winning season – for week in, week out, through the season he took with an impressive nonchalance, the hardest set of returns in the Championship. He was called 'The Panda' – he was large and dark of head and eye and adopted the stance of that curious creature. Haydn was the lively one, the charmer, the joker, the boy for the night out, even when captain Wilf Wooller disapproved. Telephoning him one night, he said: 'Skipper I've got a broken finger.' 'What are you going to do about it?' asked Wooller. 'I'll go on playing and try to keep it out of the way.'

He once claimed a catch while he was suffering from a broken thumb; that he could adjust the point in his hands at which he took the ball that only the accident of his being blinded of sight of the ball could cause him to be hit on the injured thumb.

His hitting became so celebrated throughout the land, though it lacked consistency, that many small boys preferred to watch him bat rather than collect autographs! In fact, in one match against Worcestershire at Ebbw Vale, he hit a ball pitching outside the off-stump, off the back foot, into the river at long-on. Haydn Davies revelled in the big hit, but in 1950, when pushed into opening with Gilbert Parkhouse, he scored 54 not out. He showed that day that he had the temperament to play a restrained innings, always 'down the line' with a straight bat. It was felt that during his prime in 1955 – he topped the national wicket-keeping list with 82 victims – that it was his slightly erratic exhibitions with the bat which prevented him from playing for England. There used to be a saying in cricket that in picking a cricket team you should always pick the wicket-keeper first. Glamorgan were fortunate in having their first choice to hand in Haydn Davies who between 1947 and 1957, appeared in 254 consecutive Championship games. His excellent work behind the stumps resulted in the dismissal of 782 batsmen for the County.

Haydn Davies retired at the end of 1958 and became coach at the Edinburgh Squash and Tennis Club. He returned to South Wales in the mid-1970s to run a pub in Pembrokeshire. His brother Roy, whom he legally adopted during the war, played once for Glamorgan in 1950, while his nephew Andrew Davies, won a Blue at Cambridge in 1984.

One of the finest wicket-keepers to play for Glamorgan, Haydn Davies died on 4th September, 1993 at Haverfordwest.

ROGER DAVIS

Born: 1st January, 1946. Cardiff
Played: 1964-1976

FIRST-CLASS GLAMORGAN RECORD

Innings	Not Out	Runs	H.Sc.	Average	100's
369	30	7363	134	21.71	5

Overs	Mdns	Runs	Wkts	Average	Best
2868.0	700	7793	241	32.33	6-62

NOTABLE FEATS
- He scored over 1,000 runs in a season for Glamorgan in 1975.
- He held 5 catches in an innings against Northamptonshire at Sophia Gardens in 1970.
- He held 208 catches in first-class games during his career with Glamorgan.

WHEN GLAMORGAN WON the County Championship in 1969, they had the best close-to-the-wicket group of fielders in the country in Majid, Bryan Davis, Walker, Cordle and Roger Davis – for the County has never had a more skilled or braver short square-leg than Roger Davis.

The brother of F. J. Davis, who played for Glamorgan from 1959 to 1967, he was educated at Blundell's School, before making his County debut in 1964.

Roger Davis was involved in two incidents for the County that he would probably much rather forget – he had five sixes in an over hit off his bowling as Majid Khan, then playing for Pakistan, hit 147 in the space of 89 minutes. He was also alas the Glamorgan fielder who actually 'caught' Gary Sobers on the fifth delivery of that epic Malcolm Nash over, but in doing so, fell over the long-off boundary rope and another six was signalled.

He was not averse to some big-hitting himself and in 1968, he and Bryan Davis added exactly 100 runs in less than an hour as the Glamorgan batsmen were instructed to go for quick runs in the match against the Australians – which the Welsh side won by 79 runs.

– *Famous Cricketers of Glamorgan* –

ROGER DAVIS

In the Championship winning season of 1969, he and Alan Jones put on 224 for the first wicket against Derbyshire as the County won by an innings. When he was given the opportunity to open the Glamorgan innings, Roger Davis flourished as a batsman and it was partly for this reason that the Glamorgan committee voted in favour of not retaining the services of West Indian Test star Roy Fredericks in 1974.

As a bowler, Roger Davis could make his off-spinners bite, and in 1970, he produced his best figures with the ball of six for 62 against Gloucestershire at Cheltenham.

By 1971, Roger Davis had emerged as a fearless and quite brilliant short leg. He was crouching in his usual short-leg position in the game against Warwickshire at Sophia Gardens when Neil Abberley, the Warwickshire opener, middled a leg glance off Malcolm Nash. It hit Davis a terribly sickening blow on the temple and the stricken fielder collapsed and went into violent convulsions with his legs jerking and twitching. Fortunately, there was a doctor in the member's enclosure who, on seeing the situation, sprinted out to help. On his arrival in the middle, he announced that Davis had stopped breathing and began mouth-to-mouth resuscitation. Mercifully, he started to breathe again and after about twenty minutes he was carried off the field and taken straight to hospital. The immediate news from the hospital was not good and there were fears that he may have severe brain damage. Thankfully, Davis dispelled these fears by making a full recovery and returning to the Glamorgan team by mid-August, though he never again fielded at short-leg.

In September of that season in the game against Surrey, Glamorgan were set 287 to win in five hours on a worn Oval wicket. At 232 for seven, the game was set for a Surrey win or a long defiance for a draw. For eighty minutes, Roger Davis batted out the game for 17 not out, with Surrey fielders crouched in amazingly close positions – it was a miraculous performance after that early season disaster. The 1971 season also saw Davis hit the highest score of his career, 134 against Worcestershire at Cardiff.

He had his best season with the bat in 1975 when he made 1,243 runs – having an outstanding game against Lancashire, scoring 61 and taking five for 86.

Left: Neil Hawke bowls to Roger Davis in the 1968 match at Swansea

Yet, the following season when he was going through what was his first bad patch with the County, he received a letter from the

Glamorgan committee informing him that 'the officials are deeply concerned at the quality and standard of play' and 'are not happy about your personal performance. The committee therefore felt it only right and proper that you should be advised at the earliest possible date of their opinion.' Roger Davis was, to say the least, deeply shocked and a few days later, he resigned in protest.

ARNOLD DYSON

Born: 10th July, 1905. Halifax
Died: 7th June, 1978
Played: 1926-1948

FIRST-CLASS GLAMORGAN RECORD

Innings	Not Out	Runs
696	37	17920
H.Sc.	Average	100's
208	27.19	24

Overs	Mdns	Runs	Wkts	Average	Best
34	2	160	1	160.00	1-9

NOTABLE FEATS

- He scored 208 v. Surrey at the Oval in 1932.
- He carried his bat for Glamorgan on five occasions, with a best of 191* out of 352 v. Lancashire at the Arms Park in 1934.
- He hit 104 before lunch v. Kent at Swansea in 1937 – it was also the first century of the season.
- His best season was 1938, when he scored 1,885 runs at 40.97
- He scored 1,000 runs in a season for Glamorgan on 10 occasions.

A YOUNG OPENING BATSMAN from Halifax, Arnold Dyson made his debut for Glamorgan in 1926, but did not gain a regular place in the team until 1928.

He accomplished little in his first seasons, though he did hit his maiden first-class century, 106 against Gloucestershire in 1929. Thereafter, Dyson began to display the tenacious qualities of an upbringing in the Yorkshire Leagues, as he and Emrys Davies replaced Bates and Bell as the Glamorgan opening pair.

He was a man who did not tolerate any abuse of a game for which he had a passionate zest. He was always immaculately turned out and his batting was as neat and tidy as his appearance. An orthodox player he was a particularly good driver and cutter and was never bothered by pace. Though not really considered a fast scorer he could go quick enough when necessary.

Arnold Dyson's highest score in first-class cricket came in the match against Surrey at the Oval in 1932. Surrey batted first, both Jack Hobbs and D. R. Jardine being absent, and declared at 424 for 8, with Jack Mercer performing the hat-trick. The rest of the match was dominated by the marvellous batting of Arnold Dyson. While the other batsmen kept their wickets intact, Dyson batted in steady fashion. After four hours at the wicket he reached his century, but then opened out, his score at the drawing of stumps on the second day being 186. He added only 22 runs on the Friday morning before being clean bowled by Fender, but his 208 out of 342 in 6¼ hours was an invaluable innings for his County and prevented almost certain defeat.

He missed one match during the summer of 1933, the August Bank Holiday game this breaking in the middle of his two long runs. He played in 100 consecutive matches from 1930 to 1933 and 232 consecutive matches from then to the end of the 1947 season.

During his qualifying period, he played for the Neath Club, and it was in the first county match played at Neath in 1934, that he unluckily missed the distinction of scoring a century in each innings. Essex were the visitors, Dyson scoring 96 and 104 not out. In the first innings, he was four short of his century, when he late cut a ball which flashed to the boundary; the crowd were cheering what they thought was his hundred, but they saw the batsman head for the pavilion for he had dislodged the off bail. The match with Lancashire in that same season was a triumph for Arnold Dyson. Lancashire batted into the second day, before declaring at 514 for 7 (Hopwood 123, E. Tyldesley 239) before the rest of the game was dominated by the fine batting performance of Dyson. Losing his opening partner, Emrys Davies and then Duckfield quickly, he was joined by Turnbull and a stand was made. At the close of play five wickets had fallen for 229 runs, but Dyson could find no one to stay with him and Glamorgan had to follow-on, but when the last wicket fell at 352, Dyson was still at the wicket with 91 runs on the board – a fine fighting innings.

The following season, he was involved in an unusual incident in the game against South Africa at Swansea. Louis Duffus, the South African cricket correspondent, acted as a substitute fielder and dismissed Dyson by holding a catch in the slips!

Dyson himself was also a fine close-in fielder, at slip or short-leg in what he affectionately termed 'the suicide squad'. He held 241 catches and his advanced tactical thinking on the leg-side development played a material part in Wilf Wooller's captaincy in 1948, when his theory of leg-side attack brought Glamorgan the County Championship.

In 1937, he scored a century before lunch – it was also the first of the season, coming in the match against Kent at Swansea on 1st May. That season also saw several Glamorgan records established in the match against Leicestershire. For the first time, three batsmen scored a century in an innings and a record first wicket partnership of 274 was set up by Dyson and Emrys Davies – what memory that opening partnership conjures up for Welsh cricket lovers. Outside county circles it was not generally appreciated that these two batsmen formed one of the best opening pairs in the first-class game of their day. They produced 32 opening century partnerships, with the last three in 1947 made in successive innings.

In 1938, he had his most successful season, scoring 1,885 runs at an average of 40.97. He narrowly missed recording three centuries in successive innings (94.96 and 170*) but saved one of his best performances of the summer for a friendly against Sir Julien Cahn's team for the second match of the Newport 'week'. The visitors batted first and totalled 215, but when Glamorgan batted, J. E. Walsh, the Australian, bowled with such deadly effect only Dyson, who carried his bat for 110* was able to deal with his slow left-arm bowling, that he took all nine wickets that fell, Matthews being unable to bat and thus depriving him of a record. Dyson must have created a favourable impression, for at the end of the season, he made his one tour abroad, to New Zealand with Sir Julien Cahn's team.

Against Gloucestershire at Newport in 1939, Arnold Dyson batted right through an innings for the sixth time. He scored 99 not out in the first innings and 120 in the second, thus once more narrowly missing two centuries in a match. When 99, he lost two partners in one over!

He was an admirable runner between the wickets, quick off the mark and always on the look out for that second run, especially to third man. Once in a mad run-rush against Sussex at Cardiff in 1947, Wilf Wooller instructed Dyson and Emrys Davies to go for quick runs. 'Skipper, I shall do what I always do. Treat each ball exactly on its merits. Cricket is too great a game to play as a circus.' Fortunately, as Wilf Wooller relates there was an abundance of long hops and the two batsmen put on 116 for the first wicket in 47 minutes!

Arnold Dyson died in Bradford on June 7th 1978, after a short illness. His average of 27.60 with 25 centuries in all matches was good going for a County that was propping up the championship table more often that not.

DAVID EVANS

Born: 27th July, 1933. Lambeth
Died: 25th March, 1990
Played: 1956-1969

FIRST-CLASS GLAMORGAN RECORD

Innings	Not Out	Runs	H.Sc.	Average	100's
364	91	2875	46*	10.53	0

Overs	Mdns	Runs	Wkts	Average	Best
4.0	0	12	0	–	–

NOTABLE FEATS
- He made 558 dismissals in his career with Glamorgan.
- His best season was 1963, when he helped to dismiss 89 batsmen – 78 caught and 11 stumped.
- In 1967, he captured the scalps of six Yorkshire batsmen (all caught) in an innings at Swansea.

David Evans wicket-keeping.

BORN AT LAMBETH, LONDON on July 27th 1933, David Gwilym Lloyd Evans often referred humorously to himself as a Welsh cockney. The family moved back to West Wales soon after his birth and lived at Penygroes, near Ammanford, where he played his early cricket from the age of seven. Through his primary education at Penygroes and Ammanford Valley Grammar School, his love and skill of the game of cricket developed enough for him to turn his back on a career in banking.

He graduated to the town side in the South Wales and Monmouthshire League where he was noticed by the Glamorgan committee during a benefit match against the County. Six keepers were under review and three years passed before he was invited to join the staff in 1956, making his debut against Combined Services.

In 1959, he took over as wicket-keeper after the retirement of Haydn Davies – his technical ability winning him the award of a much-treasured County cap. It was a daunting prospect to follow in the steps of the stalwart who had served the County for 23 years but he strove tirelessly for perfection, spending many hours talking and enquiring from his fellow wicket-keepers on how he could improve his own game.

He certainly proved that he was up to the task, and over the next ten years he maintained the high standards. Whether it was the left-arm pace of Jeff Jones or the sharp off-cut of Don Shepherd, he was equally at home, favouring the efficient, quiet, no-nonsense method, as opposed to the flurry of activity that spectators sometimes associate with fellow professionals.

In 1963, Glamorgan finished second in the County Championship, winning their last game of the season against Lancashire by an innings – all the Welsh side's bowlers were aided by some excellent wicket-keeping by David Evans, who broke the County record with 89 victims and became the leading wicket-keeper in the country.

He also developed into a stubborn lower-order batsman and frequently relished the job as nightwatchman; his best score of 46 not out coming against Oxford University at The Parks in 1961.

During the mid 1960s, Evans picked up several niggling injuries and was replaced by Eifion Jones who had originally joined the Glamorgan staff as a batsman. It was as the Welsh side struggled for runs that preference was increasingly given to Jones and Evans lost his place in the side. At the end of the 1967 season, he was awarded the Churchill Scholarship to travel to Australia, New Zealand, Fiji, Sri Lanka and Singapore, making everlasting friendships wherever he moved, lecturing, coaching, talking and studying cricket. The following winter, the Glamorgan office received a great many letters paying tribute to the contributions David Evans had made whilst on his travels.

With his playing career ended, he was given a benefit in 1969, and as a true Welsh-speaking Welshman, he was delighted that it coincided with the County's second Championship success.

David Evans retired from county cricket that year after 270 first-class appearances. During his career, he scored 2,875 runs at an average of 10.53 whilst behind the stumps, he caught 502 and stumped 56 victims. He coached for a while in The Hague before taking his family to Tasmania where he coached with the Northern Tasmanian Cricket Association, later joining the umpires' list in 1971.

He then graced the Test and county grounds as a T.C.C.B. umpire, exhibiting a sensitiveness and kind manner as the pressure became much more demanding. Elevated to the Test panel, his first Test happened to be the historic Ashes encounter at Headingley in 1981.

David Evans stood in eight further Tests until 1985, but was subsequently dogged by bouts of poor health, though the immense respect accorded him as an umpire was reflected in his appointment as chairman of the professional body of first-class umpires. He was always happiest at the thought of helping others and this he did by representing his colleagues at various meetings at Lord's.

He underwent a heart bypass operation and was able to resume his umpiring duties but not at Test level. In fact, he was due to stand with Kevin Lyons, his former Glamorgan colleague, in the M.C.C. v. Champion County match at the start of the 1990 season.

David Evans's love of the Welsh language enabled him to broadcast in his native togue for B.B.C. Wales, on both television and radio about his love for the game of cricket. He was also a very popular after dinner speaker and had spoken at the centenary dinner of the Radyr C.C. only two days before his untimely death.

He has been sadly missed by everyone throughout the cricket world from Test right down to club level.

ROY FREDERICKS

Born: 11th November, 1942. Blairkont, Guyana
Played: 1971-1973

FIRST-CLASS GLAMORGAN RECORD

Innings	Not Out	Runs	H.Sc.	Average	100's
80	8	2991	228*	41.54	7

Overs	Mdns	Runs	Wkts	Average	Best
207.1	45	667	20	33.35	3-37

NOTABLE FEATS

- He scored 1,000 runs in a season for Glamorgan on two occasions.
- He scored an unbeaten 228 in the match against Northamptonshire at Swansea in 1972, setting a new 1st wicket record partnership of 330 with Alan Jones.
- He scored 145* against Nottinghamshire at Trent Bridge in 1971 – his first innings for Glamorgan in a first-class match.

ROY CLINTON FREDERICKS came to the limelight in the 1966-67 Shell Shield competition when he scored 127 and 115 in the same match against Barbados, the Shield winners, and 128 not out against Jamaica. He scored 64 not out for the Board President's XI, and 57 for Guyana against M.C.C. in 1968, which earned him selection for the tour to Australia.

There he developed into a sound opening batsman and displaced his Guyanese opening partner, Steve Camacho, in the second Test, scoring 76 and 47 on his debut. He retained his place for the rest of the tour on which he scored a total of 1,055 runs for the team.

Roy Fredericks joined the County during the winter months of 1970-71 as the Welsh side sought a replacement for Bryan Davis. Other Test stars were considered, namely Alvin Kallicharran, Abid Ali, Hedley Howarth and Norbert Phillip, but it was Roy Fredericks who was chosen.

As a Test batsman, he always played well within limitations set by himself. He played in 59 Tests, scoring 4,344 runs at an average of 42.49 and a highest score of 169. This came in the second Test at Perth in 1975 as West Indies won by an innings and 87 runs. He began by hooking Dennis Lillee's second ball for six and his runs came at a bewildering pace as he hooked and drove and cut Thomson and Lillee. His hundred came in one hour fifty-six minutes off 71 balls with one six and 18 fours and when he was caught at slip off Lillee, he had made 169 out of 258.

At Lord's in 1976, he hit 138, hitting 14 fours and a six off Tony Greig in his 282 minutes innings – he had become the fifth (and last) player to score a century and a 'duck' in the same Lord's Test – the innings rounded off a splendid Lord's Test career for Fredericks, whose five innings at the ground produced scores of 63, 60, 51, 0 and 138.

Though he scored an unbeaten 145 against Nottinghamshire at Trent Bridge in his first innings for Glamorgan at the beginning of May 1971, he didn't have the best of luck, for in only his third game he broke an arm when he was hit by a ball bowled by fellow West Indian Vanburn Holder on a dangerous wicket at Sophia Gradens. In his first season with the County he failed really to show any consistency with the bat and his quite adventurous style, where his attacking instincts ran riot from the first ball, brought him lots of criticism from certain writers. They felt that a county opening batsman should be much more orthodox and push straight down the line in the early overs of a game. Yet he made attacking field placings look ridiculous and two lightning knocks of 93 and 40 put Glamorgan on the road to their first victory since May when he returned in early July.

In the one-day game though, it was a different matter altogether, and in the Sunday League game against Yorkshire at Swansea he hit a magnificent 84.

Also in that first season his left-arm wrist spin caused a few problems around the country. It was a very quick wrist action which no one could read accurately. But there was one drawback and perhaps the reason he had a modest bowling record. It took Roy three overs or so before he 'dropped' it somewhere near the spot!

In 1972, he made a career best 228 not out in the match against Northants as he and Alan Jones shared a record opening stand of 330. This innings confounded the critics who believed Fredericks was not capable of playing a long innings – however, his five hours at the crease was to no avail, as Bedi and Cottam ripped out the last seven Glamorgan wickets for the addition of just seven runs to give Northants a surprise victory by 29 runs.

During mid-June 1973, Roy Fredericks left the County to join the West Indian touring party. Yet even before his departure there were some doubts about his future with the Club. Even before the season started, the Glamorgan committee considered releasing him and sign a bowler. However, also clouding the issue was the improvement in batting from some of the young colts – though Glamorgan's other overseas player, Majid Khan, would likely to be touring England with the Pakistan team in 1974.

Eventually, a vote was taken at the general committee meeting at the Bridgend Police Club. The voting was 11-10 in favour of not retaining the West Indian and it was agreed that Fredericks be released.

The decision brought many objections and at the 1974 A.G.M., Peter Walker severely criticsed Club officials 'not only for their general approach to Fredericks, but to star players and their naive faith in local talent which is not in my view of a high enough standard to compete in the modern first-class game.'

Throughout his 80 innings for the County, Roy Fredericks found concentration very difficult, but he did play several devastating innings and I feel that Glamorgan did not make the most of their investment in him.

BERNARD HEDGES

Born: 10th November, 1927. Pontypridd
Played: 1950-1967

FIRST-CLASS GLAMORGAN RECORD

Innings	Not Out	Runs	H.Sc.	Average	100's
744	41	17733	182	25.22	21

Overs	Mdns	Runs	Wkts	Average	Best
94.0	24	260	3	86.66	1-16

NOTABLE FEATS
- He scored 1,000 runs in a season for Glamorgan on 9 occasions.
- In 1961, he scored 2,206 runs at 32.15.
- In 1962, he scored 1,851 runs at 35.59.
- He scored 103* v. Somerset at the Arms Park in the 1963 Gillette Cup Competition.

A SOUND RIGHT-HANDED batsman and fine outfield, Bernard Hedges made his first-clas debut for Glamorgan in 1950 – a season which saw him make his maiden century, 103 against Sussex in the Championship match at Chichester.

Like many Glamorgan cricketers, Hedges was a keen rugby player and played full-back for both Pontypridd and Swansea.

In 1954, the 27-year-old batsman from Pontypridd scored a century in a partnership with Gilbert Parkhouse of 219 in a comfortable win over Warwickshire at Stradey Park. The two of them developed a good understanding and the following season were the only batsmen to show any real form. He and Parkhouse continued to bat well together and in 1959, Hedges made over 1,500 runs in a season for the first time.

Though he scored 21 centuries for Glamorgan, perhaps his best innings came in the match against Lancashire in mid-July 1960. Glamorgan arrived at Aigburth, Liverpool, having lost six matches out of nine and failing to win the remaining three. Lancashire were lying second in the table and in with a good chance of the Championship – if ever there was a sure thing in cricket, this certainly looked to be it.

On winning the toss, Don Shepherd, the Glamorgan captain, decided to bat. Memories were recalled of a Welsh debacle in 1924 when on the same ground, Glamorgan had been put out for 22, the lowest score in their first-class history, especially when Lancashire had them at 25 for five. In his 17 years as a county player, Bernard Hedges never played a finer innings than the 83 he proceeded to take off Brian Statham and company. A short, but severe storm wiped out 95 minutes playing time just after Don Ward joined Hedges in what was to prove a great century stand for the sixth wicket. Ward played his part, but Hedges was the man in charge, the man of stature upon whom the events of the day hinged. On losing Ward, Hedges took upon himself the additional burden of trying to shield the tail. His anxiety to get Brian Evans away from the bowling caused him to pick the wrong ball to attempt a forcing stroke off Roy Collins and he was bowled 17 runs short of what would have been a magnificent century – batting for 3 hours 20 minutes, it must have been a great disappointment to him that he was unable to set the three figure seal upon the greatest innings of his life. It provided a remarkable turn around, for Glamorgan went on to win by 50 runs.

The following season, he passed 2,000 runs in all first-class matches for the first time in his career and was awarded a well deserved benefit season in 1963. In 1962, he topped the 1,800 run mark to help the County to its handful of victories that season.

In 1963 in the Club's inaugural one-day game against Somerset at Cardiff, Bernard Hedges hit an unbeaten 103 as Glamorgan totalled 207 for eight at the end of their alloted 60 overs in the Gillette Cup – and went on to win by ten runs.

A very good servant of the Club, Bernard Hedges scored 17,733 runs for the County over his 17 years in the first-class game.

JOHN HOPKINS

Born: 16th June, 1953. Maesteg
Played: 1970-1988

FIRST-CLASS GLAMORGAN RECORD

Innings	Not Out	Runs	H.Sc.	Average	100's
524	32	13610	230	27.66	18

Overs	Mdns	Runs	Wkts	Average	Best
26.0	3	148	0	–	–

NOTABLE FEATS
- He held 5 catches in an innings v. Worcestershire at Sophia Gardens in 1976.
- He scored 230 v. Worcestershire at Worcester in 1977.
- He score 1,000 runs in a season for Glamorgan on 7 occasions.
- He scored 103* v. Minor Counties at Swansea in the 1980 Benson and Hedges Cup competition.
- He scored 130* v. Somerset at Bath in the 1983 Sunday League.
- In 1983, he carried his bat for 109* out of 240 v. Derbyshire at Swansea.

JOHN HOPKINS was born in Maesteg, second in a family of five sporting brothers. The eldest brother, Jeffries, was understudy to Middlesex's John Murray at Lord's for a number of years, whilst a younger brother, Ken, gained a rugby blue at full-back for Oxford in 1978.

In his early years John came under the watchful eye of the late Cyril Evans, who coached and developed so many promising young cricketers for the Welsh County.

His potential was noted in 1970, when at the age of 17 and on the Lord's groundstaff, he made his first-class debut for Glamorgan in the match against Gloucestershire at Colwyn Bay. Amongst the distinguished company of Majid Khan, Tony Lewis and Peter Walker, he hit 88 in an innings of maturity.

– *Famous Cricketers of Glamorgan* –

JOHN HOPKINS

For the following six years he only played on a part-time basis whilst qualifying for a teaching certificate at Trinity College, Carmarthen and then working in local schools. However, it didn't stop him from scoring his maiden century in 1976, when he made 105 against Warwickshire at Edgbaston.

In 1977, his first full season, he made a magnificent 230 in the match against Worcestershire at New Road in an innings lasting 6¾ hours. He hit 26 fours to register the highest post-war score for the County, as Glamorgan won by eight wickets. It was an innings that greatly impressed many people, including Norman Gifford, who was then in the Worcester side. That season saw Glamorgan beat Leicestershire in the Gillette Cup semi-finals at Swansea in a match that took three days to complete, to go through to Lord's to play Middlesex in the final.

John Hopkins was enjoying a splendid season and in the final played with the good sense expected of one who had recently been awarded his County cap. He played some crisp shots that did not always bring the runs they deserved. Losing Jones, King and Ontong, he and Llewellyn revived the County's hopes, before he was bowled by Phil Edmonds for 47.

Following his success that summer, he was awarded a Whitbread Scholarship in the winter of 1977-78, and was sent to a local club in Melbourne. Unfortunately, due to a serious family illness, he had to return home to Maesteg and experienced just a few months of cricket in Australia. The following spring, he was selected to play for the M.C.C. against Pakistan at Lord's, but failed to make any impression and did not get another chance.

John Hopkins was an all-round sportsman, playing centre-threequarter for his college – coming from the close knit mining community of the Llynfi Valley, it is not too surprising. One of the old school, he still enjoyed his pint of lager and a song or two at the end of a game.

Had he moved on to another county early in his career, he would most certainly have gained higher honours, especially at one-day level. In 1980, he hit an unbeaten 103 against the Minor Counties in the Benson and Hedges Cup, whilst three years later, he scored 130 not out in the Refuge Assurance League match against Somerset at Bath. However, in 1984, he must have come very close to full England honours – it was his best season, as he scored 1,500 runs at an average of 33.33. It was a summer when England were wondering who to turn to next to open the batting against the West Indies. He had taken a gritty 40 odd off the Notts attack of Hadlee, Rice and Saxelby on a 'helpful' Trent Bridge wicket, whilst a couple of weeks later, he scored 74 at Hove in the match against Sussex, with the ball swinging and lifting. In fact, a few days before the second Test, England Selector Peter May had mentioned that they were looking for an opener with a sound technique and who was currently in form – John Hopkins, who was averaging 40 plus at the time, was as experienced if not more so than most of the country's openers. He never got his chance, and like Alan Jones and Don Shepherd before him, never got the recognition he deserved.

Like another prolific Glamorgan opening batsman, Gilbert Parkhouse, John Hopkins spent his time in the field at slip – perhaps his liking for this position stemmed from his early days as an extremely competent wicket-keeper – taking 210 catches during his 18 year career. He did captain Glamorgan on one occasion when both Mike Selvey and Rodney Ontong, the vice-captain, were injured and did it competently and professionally, as one would expect.

A model professional, one of his greatest attributes was his determination – for he helped Glamorgan through countless crises! Alan Jones, Hopkins's opening partner for seven seasons summed up this ideal man for any situation: 'He's a fighter, he has a big heart and if my life depended on it, I would always have John Hopkins.'

JAVED MIANDAD

Born: 12th June, 1957. Karachi
Played: 1980-1986

FIRST-CLASS GLAMORGAN RECORD

Innings	Not Out	Runs	H.Sc.	Average	100's
135	22	6531	212*	57.80	17

Overs	Mdns	Runs	Wkts	Average	Best
254.3	57	851	21	40.52	3-52

NOTABLE FEATS
- He scored 140* v. Essex at Swansea in 1980 – his first innings for Glamorgan.
- He carried his bat for 131* out of 181 v. Warwickshire at Edgbaston in 1980.

- His best season was 1981, when he scored 2,083 runs at an average of 69.43, including eight hundreds.
- He scored 200* on three occasions: v. Somerset at Taunton and v. Essex at Castle Park, Colchester, both in 1981 and v. Australia at Neath in 1985.
- He hit three centuries in successive innings in 1981: 105 v. Warwickshire and 137* and 106 v Somerset both at Swansea.
- He took 28 runs off an over from Warwickshire's Asif Din at the Sophia Gardens in 1981.
- He scored 1,000 runs in a season for Glamorgan on three occasions.
- He scored 212* v. Leicestershire at Swansea in 1984.
- He shares the Glamorgan 4th wicket record partnership with Younis Ahmed of 306* v. Australians at Neath in 1985.

THE HIGHEST RUN-SCORER in Pakistan's Test history, he came into first-class cricket (for Karachi Whites) when he was 16, while a few months later, he scored 311 for them against the National Bank. His promise was such that Sussex rushed to recruit him. While he was still qualifying for the county and barely 18, he struck 227 runs for the second eleven in their match with Hampshire – amazing the opposition with his brilliance.

At 19, he became only the second player to score a century in his first Test innings for Pakistan and less than a month later, he became the youngest to score a double century in Test cricket. At 22, he was made captain of his country – far too young, for his volatile personality got him involved in a fiery scene with Dennis Lillee when Pakistan toured Australia in 1981-82.

In 1980, Sussex found their list of overseas players too long and so he joined Glamorgan with instant and sustained success.

He produced some devastating performances, hitting an unbeaten 140 in the opening Championship match against Essex and another in the following match against Gloucestershire, as Glamorgan won their first match in the Championship for two years. Yet, there was one problem.

When Miandad first came to Britain, he could barely utter a word in English. Coaching from his friend Sadiq Mohammed, and life with the Sussex players, finally overcame that, but on joining Glamorgan he had to contend with an entirely new accent!

As Malcolm Nash said: 'Javed makes himself understood to us well enough – but I think he has a fair bit of difficulty making out the Welsh tongue at the moment. Most of us in the side can speak Welsh, and it is occasionally useful to chatter in, especially on the field when you don't want the opposition to understand!'

He had a marvellous season in 1981, amassing a Club record of 2,083 runs to finish with an average of 69.43, the best ever by a Glamorgan batsman. He hit eight centuries including two double-centuries. His unbeaten 200 at Colchester in the match against Essex was one of the finest innings many of his colleagues had ever seen. Chasing 325 in 323 minutes, they lost Alan Jones without a run on the board, and though the wicket was giving considerable help to the spinners, Miandad hit 22 boundaries to take Glamorgan to the verge of victory. Unfortunately, no one else could stay with him and he was left unbeaten as the Welsh side fell 14 runs short of what would have been a wonderful victory.

As a batsman Miandad was confident, perhaps even arrogant. It had not made him the most popular of opponents, but he does believe that he was good enough to dominate any attack. Few, if any, of the world's top batsmen pick length better and then react more swiftly. He could turn a good length ball into half-volley with one of his typical darts down the pitch. A safe and economical player of the fastest bowling, he was also one of the most difficult players in the world to contain for the slow bowler. He refused to be tied to his crease, but when he choose to stay he would cut and sweep into the gaps with great precision.

Javed Miandad has never felt bound by the text book – he was the game's premier inventor.

After a few seasons of debate of who the side's overseas player should be, most supporters were delighted when it was resolved that Jazved should play in 1985.

He responded by scoring a cetury in the opening Championship match of the season at the Oval, guiding Glamorgan to a seven-wicket win. In the next match, he hit 86 in quickfire time as the Welsh side defeated Somerset by nine wickets. His finest moment of the season came in the match at the Gnoll against the Australian tourists. He made a faultless unbeaten double century, reaching his 200 with a towering six onto the Mayor of Neath's marquee alongside the pavilion. Together with Younis Ahmed, he added 306, the highest by any county side for the fourth wicket against Australia. Both Pakistani batsmen presented their bats to the Neath Club, where they hang today, alongside the one used by W. G. Grace who, when he played at Neath in 1868, bagged a pair!

He also made a great personal contribution in the Sunday League, scoring a record 573 runs at an average of 63.37.

In 1986, the re-engagement of Ezra Moseley upset Miandad, who was unhappy at the prospect of playing on a rota system again. He wanted a new three-year contract, but the Club couldn't meet his wishes, and informed him that they expected him to be available for 1986, during which a review of his future would be made.

However, during April in Sharjah, he helped Pakistan to win the inaugural Five-Nation Australasia Cup, his innings of 116 not out being climaxed by a six off the last ball of the match and failed to return for the opening matches of the season. In fact, he later telephoned Philip Carling from Lahore and said: 'It seems that I am only required to play for part of the season. My future does not rest with Glamorgan. It is here in Pakistan.' In mid-season, he returned to Swansea to collect his belongings from his home in South Wales and sell the house. While he was here, he made an attempt to be re-instated, but the Glamorgan committee felt that the Pakistani had let them down and his request, was turned down.

Just three days after his late arrival in England in May 1987, he scored 211 not out for Pakistan against Sussex, but the fact remained that when the final Test of the summer began at the Oval, the impish man with the dark hair and moustache, was still awaiting his first Test century against England. Coming in on the first morning at 45 for two, he batted ten hours and 17 minutes to make 260. It was not his highest score in Test cricket, but perhaps his most dominant innings.

ALAN JONES

Born: 4th November, 1938. Velindre
Played: 1957-1983

FIRST-CLASS GLAMORGAN RECORD

Innings	Not Out	Runs	H.Sc.	Average	100's
1102	71	34056	204*	33.03	52

Overs	Mdns	Runs	Wkts	Average	Best
58.5	15	249	1	249.00	1-41

NOTABLE FEATS
- He scored a hundred in each innings of a match on three occasions: 187* and 105* v. Somerset at Glastonbury in 1963; 132 and 156* v. Yorkshire at Middlesbrough in 1976 and 147 and 100 v. Hampshire at Swansea in 1978.
- He scored 1,000 runs in a season for Glamorgan on 23 occasions.
- His best season was 1966, when he scored 1,865 runs at 34.53, though the previous season had seen him score 1,805 runs at 38.40.
- He shares with Roy Fredericks, the Glamorgan first-wicket record partnership of 330 v Northamptonshire at Swansea in 1972.
- He holds the Glamorgan first-wicket record partnership in all one-day competitions.
- He scored 204* v. Hampshire at Basingstoke in 1980.
- He is the leading run-getter for Glamorgan in all three one-day competitions.

A LAN JONES M.B.E. was a Glamorgan cricketer through and through, and Welsh to his fingertips.

Born at Velindre, son of a West Wales miner, he grew up in a sporting atmosphere with kindly parents who encouraged their nine sons to play games. Most of the brothers played for the Clydach Club in the South Wales Cricket Association's competition of four divisions. Alan and his brother, Eifion, graduated to

– *Famous Cricketers of Glamorgan* –

ALAN JONES

Glamorgan from the Club via the County's coaching scheme under the direction of former opening batsman, Phil Clift. When 17 years of age, Alan was drafted into the Glamorgan Colts side, where he developed under the guidance of Clift and became a first team member in 1957, beginning with a duck at Bristol.

It was reported during his first year as a professional with the County that 'his stroke play was rather limited as a result of concentration upon strengthening his defence.' However, as soon as he began to settle as a professional, he was whisked away to do two years military service in 1958-59, and had to be content playing with the Combined Services. Jones returned to the County in 1960, with a weakness around leg-stump – tending to fall away a little to the offside. Wilf Wooller, his first County captain, sorted that out for him – taking him for endless sessions in the nets, bowling in-swingers and out-swingers at him. By 1962, he had scored his maiden century in first-class cricket to win his County cap and with this innings he convinced his mentors of his ability as a stroke-maker.

However, early in the 1963 season, Alan was going through a bad patch and Ossie Wheatley, Glamorgan's captain, told him he wouldn't be playing in the match against Somerset at Glastonbury. Gilbert Parkhouse was feeling unwell on the morning of the match though, and Alan, who'd been batting at number three, was brought back into the side to open with Bernard Hedges. He hit a magnificent 187 not out in the first innings and an unbeaten 105 in the second, being on the field for every single ball of the game. He continued this fine form when the West Indian tourists visited Swansea, hooking Wes Hall for a six and numerous fours in an innings of 92. Jones was now among the young players ready to bid for an England cap – opposing bowlers began to respect him as much as Glamorgan depended upon him for a good start to each innings.

By 1966, he was taking things out on the West Indies and Wes Hall again, hooking him out of sight at St Helen's for 161 not out. He played the attacking innings of a lifetime at Cardiff in 1968 against Lancashire. Tony Lewis had declared behind on the first innings, and Jack Bond had delayed his in the third until it looked as though he had ruled Glamorgan out of the match. It wasn't a dashing declaration – the Welsh County were set 178 to win in 130 minutes on a poor wicket. Jones destroyed both Ken Higgs and

Ken Shuttleworth with a crashing innings of 95 not out which enabled Glamorgan to win by four wickets with three balls left. He was in brilliant form in the match against the Australians at St Helen's. He had made 99, when he holed out on the mid-on boundary after being lured down the track by Ashley Mallett – Glamorgan winning by 79 runs.

In 1970, though suffering from back trouble, Jones began the season with centuries against Hampshire and Worcestershire and was on the verge of making 1,000 runs in May. His outstanding form earned him a deserved place in the England side against The Rest of the World in the first 'Test' at Lord's. It did not show him at his best – Wisden said that he 'seemed overcome by the occasion'. He scored 5 and 0, each time caught at the wicket off Mike Procter, and he made way for Cowdrey for the next match – and that effectively, was that. It was Jones's first appearance for England and he was duly awarded his cap and blazer, as were all England players in that splendid series. He could well have been chosen for England before, and could well have been afterwards, but as it happened, he was not.

Worse still, Wisden erased all the caps won in that series from official Test records, not because its editor wanted to, but because the International Cricket Conference said they should not stand as official. These matches at the time were broadcast and sold as Test matches, not least by Guinness, who sponsored them on that understanding – Gary Sobers only agreed to play if they were played as Test matches!

Alan still finds it hard to understand how anyone can be given just one chance and then be totally dismissed. If the game has any honour, I feel that he should be reinstated as a Test player.

There have been various reasons offered for his omission from England teams, among them, his lack of a strong throwing arm. In fact, he had a powerful throw until 1963, when he threw his shoulder out while playing for Western Australia. There is no doubt that Alan Jones would have reached a higher peak and played regularly for England if he had been playing for another county. The pitches at Cardiff and Swansea were often fabricated for spin bowling. The move to Sophia Gardens produced a new square but of uneven bounce. Yet the wicket at St Helen's, Swansea, has been a fine wicket for some years and in 1972, he and Roy Fredericks shared a record opening stand of 330 against Northants there – the West Indian making a career best 228 not out.

Alan Jones took over the captaincy of Glamorgan in mid June 1976 and though he tried his best, there was only one Championship win in the remaining weeks under his leadership. There were few good players around him, but he still led them to the Gillette Cup Final in 1977 for the first time in the Club's history. That year, he was one of the Wisden's 'Five Cricketers of the Year', not the only man to receive this high honour who was better than many frequent England choices who did not! At the end of the following season, the Glamorgan committee opted for a new leader, though Jones had done a reasonable job and had the confidence and support of the rest of the team in difficult times. The increasing responsibility may have made him less attractive, but he never flinched from it. He did not have a particularly strong physique and would sometimes be in pain after a long innings.

In 1980, he hit an unbeaten 204 in the match against Hampshire at Basingstoke – it was his 50th first-class hundred, the highest score of his career and his first double-century. He began the 1982 season with the first first-class century of the season – 103 against Cambridge University at Fenner's – to bring his overall total of hundreds to 52.

As a batsman he combined a fine technique with admirable powers of concentration.

He was a model for the youngsters in the Welsh side and for the players in the Second Eleven, whom he coached after his retirement in 1983. He was justifiably rewarded with the award of the M.B.E. in the Birthday Honours List for his services to Glamorgan cricket – to a Welsh-speaking Welshman, it came as both a surprise and a delight.

He retired with 34,056 runs to his name, scoring over 1,000 runs in 23 consecutive seasons since 1961 – the highest scoring batsman in the game never to have played in an official Test match.

EIFION JONES

Born: 25th June, 1942. Velindre
Played: 1961-1983

FIRST-CLASS GLAMORGAN RECORD

Innings	Not Out	Runs	H.Sc.	Average	100's
591	119	8341	146*	17.67	3

Overs	Mdns	Runs	Wkts	Average	Best
0.3	0	5	0	–	–

NOTABLE FEATS

- He holds the Glamorgan record for the most dismissals in an innings of a first-class match – 7 v. Cambridge University at Cambridge in 1970.
- He holds the Glamorgan record for the most dismissals in first-class games in a season – 94 in 1970.
- He holds the record for the most dismissals in a career in first-class games for Glamorgan with 933 (840 caught, 93 stumped).

ONE OF GLAMORGAN'S finest wicket-keepers, Eifion Wyn Jones was born at Velindre near Swansea on 25th June 1942, one of a family of nine boys and two girls. His early sporting interests were kindled by his father, Wil, Efion's consuming passions became cricket and rugby football. He was in his day, a very useful rugby centre for Pontardulais in the West Wales League – his powerful stocky frame also making him ideal for the position of wicket-keeper.

However, when Eifion Jones came to Glamorgan as a Young Colt he was more interested in batting than in wicket-keeping, but travelling to the indoor nets at Neath with brother Alan, he came under the watchful eye of the then County coach, Phil Clift. There was something about his stocky stature and quick alert movements that suggested to Clift that Eifion might make a wicket-keeper.

– Famous Cricketers of Glamorgan –

EIFION JONES

And so it proved, for Eifion was a natural. In no time at all he became understudy to David Evans, but it wasn't the happiest of positions for him to be in. He was waiting in the wings for the star keeper to retire or otherwise, the best that could be hoped for was limited first-class experience when the main keeper was ill or perhaps when he was given a game in a friendly.

Eifion made his first-class debut against Nottinghamshire at Trent Bridge on 17th June 1961. He held three catches in a six-wicket victory for Glamorgan, but did not become the regular wicket-keeper for the County until 1968 and then he was probably a little fortunate that his batting carried the day, for David Evans was keeping as well as ever.

He received some early advice from the former Surrey and England wicket-keeper, Arthur McIntyre, when Glamorgan played at the Oval late that summer. Then David Evans became a guiding influence as Eifion took over as the County's first choice. He didn't consciously model himself on anyone, though Keith Andrew, formerly of Northamptonshire and England was in his mind, the best.

In 1968, he became the first Glamorgan wicket-keeper to score over 800 runs in a season since Tom Brierley. It was also the season in which he made his maiden century. He batted through the day with brother Alan at Hove against Sussex when they put on 230 undefeated in the last innings – Eifion reached his top score of 146, also undefeated.

During that summer, the County defeated Australia in a wonderful game of cricket at Swansea. Batting first, Glamorgan scored 224 and removed five Australian batsmen on the Saturday evening in a sensational spell.

On the Sunday, Eifion took two excellent catches to remove Gleeson and Mallett off Malcolm Nash as Australia were dismissed for 110. Declaring at 250 for 9, Australia were set 365 to win on an excellent Swansea wicket. The Glamorgan attack eventually won the day, helped by Jones catching Cowper and assisting in the run-out of both Redpath and Mallett – Glamorgan winning by 79 runs.

In 1969, the year when Glamorgan won the County Championship for the second time, Efion Jones had a memorable season. He was top of the County wicket-keepers with 74 victims (68 caught, 6 stumped) – a splendid achievement. That year his batting was a tremendous boost to the lower middle-order.

Against Middlesex when the result was in doubt up to the last over of the final 20, Eifion, who finished with 37 runs, hit a magnificent six to enable the County to win by three wickets. A couple of weeks later, he hit a sparkling 28 which enabled Glamorgan to declare against Essex in a game which was won off the very last ball when Ossie Wheatley hurled the ball in from third man to Jones and Lever was run out to bring victory by a single run. A win over Worcestershire or Surrey in the last two matches of the season would give Glamorgan the title. A crowd of over 10,000 entered Sophia Gradens to see the home side make 265, whilst Worcestershire could only reply with 183. Tony Lewis instructed his men to go for quick runs – Eifion making 39 in quickfire time with some ripping square-drives, before being hit on the head by Vanburn Holder and helped off into the Glamorgan dressing room. The medical opinion was that he should rest, but the loyal keper did not want to miss out and took his place behind the stumps as the visitors were dismissed 147 runs short of their target. The County had won the Championship, but all the phlegmatic Eifion would permit himself was a quiet smile!

In 1970, he created a new County record with 94 victims (85 caught, 9 stumped).

In the match against Cambridge he helped dismiss seven University batsmen in an innings to establish another County record, and came very close to selection for the M.C.C.'s winter tour of Australia. He was given a one-year contract and awarded a Testimonial for 1984, but was told that it was highly likely that Terry Davies, a 23-year old from St Albans would be the first-team wicket-keeper.

Whilst he scored 8,341 runs at 17.67, with three centuries, it is as a wicket-keeper that Eifion broke Glamorgan records. His career record of 933 dismissals – 840 catches and 93 stumpings – is a County record. In fact, it was only the consistency of Kent's Alan Knott in the early 1970s that denied him representative honours.

Eifion's consistency and model professionalism made him one of the most respected players in the game and had the Welsh county had a faster attack throughout his career he would surely have snapped up even more victims than he did behind the stumps.

JEFF JONES

Born: 10th December, 1941. Dafen
Played: 1960-1968

FIRST-CLASS GLAMORGAN RECORD

Innings	Not Out	Runs	H.Sc.	Average	100's
180	69	395	20	3.55	–

Overs	Mdns	Runs	Wkts	Average	Best
3904.4	979	9583	408	23.48	8-11

NOTABLE FEATS
- He performed the hat-trick v. Yorkshire at Harrogate in 1962.
- He took eight for 11 v. Leicestershire at Grace Road in 1965.

A TRUE SON OF THE West – that is what they called Jeff Jones in Wales – a tall, strongly built left-arm fast-medium bowler with an easy approach and high rhythmic action.

Jeff Jones was born in the West Wales village of Dafen, near the rugby town of Llanelli, on December 10th 1941. He grew into a tall, lanky lad and was soon encouraged by the village club, no mean performers in the South Wales and Monmouthshire League. In 1957, before Jeff had reached the age of 16, the local cricket secretary wrote to Glamorgan and suggested that club officials should take a look at a fast left-arm bowler of promise.

Phil Clift, the County coach, and an expert judge of young players, visited Dafen and saw young Jones in action. Even at that early age, he looked a cricketer and was fairly nippy and accurate for one so young. There was material here though Clift, worthy of encouragement and moulding, and he recommended to the County selection committee that Jones should be given a winter in the nets of the indoor school and perhaps a summer engagement in 1958.

At the age of $16\frac{1}{2}$, Jones joined the County staff and under the watchful eyes of Wilf Wooller and Phil Clift, bowled his way through the Colts, Club and Ground and Second XI's to play his first match for the County 1st XI in 1960.

With careful nursing and direction, Jones increased his wicket-taking per seasons as follows: 1960 (19) 1961 (25) 1962 (48) when he performed the hat-trick against Yorkshire at Harrogate and 1963 (58). Anyone who saw him bowl during this latter season were left in no doubt that here was an England fast bowler in the making.

During the winter of 1963-64, Jones was selected for the M.C.C. tour of India as an experiment to see if he would develop quickly and be ready to replace the great pace bowlers of the era. In fact, by playing in the second Test at Bombay, he won an England cap before he was awarded his County cap. Though he failed to take a wicket in that match and only nine in the short ten-match tour, Wisden's correspondent remarked: 'The venture was a valuable experience. He showed the will to improve and had the run-up and action necessary for success as a fast bowler.'

The tour in fact nearly ruined Jones's career as a first-class bowler, for in the summer of 1964 he fell away. The Glamorgan Year Book of 1965 recording the efforts of the previous summer stated: 'Jones troubled by an ankle injury, never settled into the bowling rhythm which promised so much in the preceding year.'

So the summer of 1965 one of decision for the gentle quiet-voiced young bowler from Dafen, and before it, the Glamorgan secretary, coach and captain 'worked' on him during the winter of 1964-65 to straighten him out and restore his smooth action as well as inducing more devil and the right delivery line. Jones accepted the advice readily, and despite a slow start to the 1965 season, he grew in pace and stature as Glamorgan's bid for the Championship gathered momentum. He captured 84 wickets in the season and in the match against Leicestershire at Grace Road, turned in his best-ever figures. Rain had interrupted play over the first two days and a draw seemed likely when Leicestershire began their second innings on the final day just 68 runs behind. However, Jeff Jones bowled fast and straight on the damp wicket and at one time, the home side were 3 for five, with all the victims falling to Jones, without the left-armer conceding a run! Though Leicestershire recovered slightly, they were all out for 40, with Jones's final figures being:

O.	M.	R.	W.
13	9	11	8

Selection for the M.C.C. tour of Australia and New Zealand followed and his captain, O. S. Wheatley, forecast that Jones would not play in the first Test against Australia, but in the remaining four Jones did exactly this, and with distinction.

He started by being barred by the umpire from bowling against New South Wales after running down the wicket. He worked hard at his follow-through and won a place in the England side for the second Test at Melbourne. He captured the wickets of the first four batsmen and went on to produce his best-ever Test figures of six for 118 in a total of 550-plus at Adelaide compiled by a rather useful batting line-up – Ian Chappell was at six and Keith Stackpole at seven.

As the only Welsh fast bowler to tour Australia, he was much in demand from his countrymen in exile, but he was often embarrassed – for people assumed that as he was from Llanelli he could speak Welsh – but Jeff had to own up and admit he couldn't speak the language! His proudest moment on the tour was when the news came through that Wales had beaten England at Twickenham in January. The call of rugby reached him even in the heat of an Australian dressing room – he was the proudest man in Australia!

Although Jeff's batting ability can be realistically assessed by a career average of 3.97, which was assisted by 84 'not outs', he did survive an over from West Indies' Lance Gibbs in his final Test to enable England to salvage a draw and win the series. But even as he played out that tumultuous last over he was carrying the injury that ended his career. He had been fielding just behind square and in attempting to save the one, flicked in a throw from the wrist and felt something go in his elbow. Mentioning it to John Snow, he was told not to worry too much about it, for he had five weeks rest at the end of the tour and that would settle it!

The year of 1968 proved to be a bad one for the 26-year-old, as he damaged ligaments in his elbow and shoulder in the match against Essex at Ilford in early June. Worse was to follow when a specialist found a mild arthritic condition in the elbow joint plus a wearing of the bone structure. He did try to make a comeback in the Glamorgan 2nd XI in the last few weeks of the season but the injury had affected his smooth bowling action and he wasn't able to bowl properly.

The Test selectors showed their appreciation of his efforts in the Caribbean by keeping a place for him in the team to go to Pakistan in the winter. Jeff was absolutely delighted when the pain disappeared and he seemed to be over the worst, but it went again and after a net session, he realised there was no way he could carry on.

The thoughts of what might have been are impossible to eliminate, for he bowled most dangerously on hard pitches, and some of his sharpest performances were overseas. His angle of delivery made evasion difficult, and among those who failed to escape the Welshman's lifters were Terry Jarvis, whose face needed fourteen stitches and Rohan Kanhai, whose cap flew off as he was hit over the heart.

Although his first-class career ended in 1969, his involvement in the game continued. When he was no-balled for throwing in the early 1970s after coming back to club cricket it looked as if misfortune was following him, but Micky Stewart came down and saw that there was nothing wrong with his delivery. Jeff even came back briefly to international cricket when Wales stood in for Gibraltar in the 1979 I.C.C. Trophy, but despite his successes for Dafen Welfare and Pontardulais, he had no thoughts of even a one-day county comeback.

Playing regularly in the Old England XI, he now represents Felinfoel, the village for whose brewery he works as an area representative, batting at No. 4!

– Famous Cricketers of Glamorgan –

WILLIE JONES

Born: 31st October, 1916. Carmarthen
Played: 1937-1958

FIRST-CLASS GLAMORGAN RECORD

Innings	Not Out	Runs	H.Sc.	Average	100's
555	63	13270	212*	27.00	11

Overs	Mdns	Runs	Wkts	Average	Best
1926.2	438	5620	189	29.73	5-50

NOTABLE FEATS
- He scored 1,000 runs in a season for Glamorgan on 7 occasions.
- In 1948, he reached 1,000 runs on 23rd June, the second earliest time.
- He scored 207 v. Kent at Gravesend in 1948.
- He scored an unbeaten 212 v. Essex at Brentwood in the same season.
- He shares the Glamorgan third-wicket partnership record of 313 with Emrys Davies v. Essex at Brentwood in that match.
- He shares the Glamorgan sixth-wicket partnership record of 230 with Bernard Muncer v. Worcestershire at Worcester in 1953.

IT WAS CERTAINLY SAID of Willie Jones that had he possessed confidence in his own natural ability, he would have joined those Glamorgan players who have represented England.

His occasional apprehensions stemmed from a fierce Welsh pride with its in-built horror of failure, but most of all from his background in the South Wales of the 1920s and 1930s, with its industrial depression and unemployment.

Despite his richly promising appearances for Glamorgan as an amateur during those years of the late 1930s, his obsession with security was such that the County club were not able to persuade him to exchange his job as road maintenance man with the Carmarthenshire County Council for a career as a professional cricketer until after the war.

– Famous Cricketers of Glamorgan –

Making his Glamorgan debut in 1937, he turned up carrying only his flannels, for he had no idea that county players were expected to provide their own playing gear. Willie just thought he helped himself to bat, pads and gloves from the bag, as he did when he played for the County Council! But Maurice Turnbull was very understanding and presented Willie with some of his own gear and a leather cricket bag in which to keep it. It was during his first season that he shared in a brilliant partnership of 153 for the third wicket with Maurice Turnbull in the match against Essex at Westcliff. It was here that he showed for the first time the flashing square-cut and the powerful off-drive that was to bring many more runs in an innings of 74.

Despite his diminuitive frame Willie Jones was a giant on the Rugby field. It was his misfortune, however, that his career as an outside-half coincided with those of Cliff Jones and W. T. H. Davies, which meant he had to be content with one 'unofficial' wartime international against England as his only reward for the many occasions he was a Welsh reserve in peacetime. He dropped many goals first for Neath and then his adopted Gloucester and Gloucestershire with such regularity, that legend has it, he was the cause of the drop goal being devalued from four points to three!

In 1946, he hit nine half-centuries, but strangely no hundreds, yet he still managed to score 1,114 runs. This had been a personal target for the little Carmarthen left-hander and as his aggregate approached the four-figure mark, he became very jittery when going out to bat. The target weighed so heavily on his mind, that rumour has it, when he was asleep at night, he would nudge his wife in bed and say 'run up, there's three here!'

His highest score that summer was 99, but the following season, he made his first hundred for the County, 132 against Essex as Glamorgan won by an innings and 53 runs. Always grateful for the kindness shown by his senior professional colleagues, he remembers Arnold Dyson coming up to him as he relaxed in the shower afterwards and hand him a £1 note, saying 'Here lad, that's to help you buy the round they'll be expecting.'

The bean-sized batsman topped the County batting averages during the summer of 1948 with 1,656 runs at 40.39 – his contribution to the County's first Championship triumph being crucial. Amazingly, he hit two double centuries, but no single centuries.

Welsh-speaking Willie had to be encouraged and bolstered. He never went to the wicket without trembling, scarcely believing that he was capable of doing the things he did. Jones played his favoured square-cut to great effect, for at Gravesend against Kent in June, he scored 207. When he came in after batting, his hand was shaking so much he could hardly hold a glass of orange squash – 'I'll never be able to do that again, skipper' he said to Wilf Wooller – but a few days later, he did it again – 212 not out against Essex at Brentwood, with Emrys Davies getting 215 in a total of 586 for five declared. He also took 47 wickets (at 25.53) that summer, mostly stand-breaking wickets, taken with left-arm slows, which caused the batsman more problems than was recognisable from the boundary edge. In fact, Somerset crumpled to his diminuitive spin, as did Hampshire, who scored a hundred in an hour going for victory, but were then dismissed in the next hour, mostly by the flighted left-arm spin of Willie Jones.

He appeared in the 1949 Test trial, but was then injured and missed the rest of the season.

One of the most attractive and punishing batsmen in the country, he remembered the advice given him by Emrys Davies during the match with the West Indies at Swansea in 1950. Worried about his ability to 'pick' Sonny Ramadhin, he was met with the reply, 'Don't worry. Neither can I, so just keep pushing forward when you're in doubt.' He had had his cap knocked off first ball by a bouncer from the West Indies' fast bowler Prior Jones, but went on to thrill a 32,000 August Bank Holiday crowd with a magnificent innings of 105.

He also remembers that hard taskmaster Wilf Wooller who, after Willie had once run out the great Len Hutton for 99 with a typical hurtling throw from the deep, astonished him with his rebuke: 'What the hell did you do that for?' Willie adding: 'He was joking of course!'

'Willie Bach', as he was affectionately known among his Welsh compatriots, had his benefit season in 1953 when he scored over 1,200 runs, but after the Championship year and until his retirement in 1958, his career was dogged by the lasting effects of a serious knee injury.

GEORGE LAVIS

Born: 17th August, 1908. Sebastopol
Died: 29th July, 1956
Played: 1928-1949

FIRST-CLASS GLAMORGAN RECORD

Innings	Not Out	Runs	H.Sc.	Average	100's
312	43	4957	154	18.42	3

Overs	Mdns	Runs	Wkts	Average	Best
2741	515	7768	156	49-79	4-55

NOTABLE FEATS
- He hit the highest score of his first-class career, 154 v. Worcestershire as he and Cyril Smart added 263 for the fourth wicket to establish a new Glamorgan record.

As a CRICKETER, George Lavis must be judged not on figures, but on actual performance. Lavis's statistics convey very inadequately the technical culture of his batting. For when George Lavis executed the cover-drive, one could be sure that it was according to the text book. He joined Glamorgan when he was 17 and was with them to the end of his days, apart from two years in Scottish cricket. It was in 1928 that George Lavis first played for the Welsh Club, but five years later before he hit his maiden first-class century, 115 against Worcestershire at Stradey Park, Llanelli – a county match being played there for the first time. In fact, it was Glamorgan's only win of the season as they won by an innings and 84 runs.

The summer of 1934 was his best season in terms of the number of runs scored – 883 at 25.22. Against Surrey at the Oval, he and Jack Mercer added 120 for the last wicket, Lavis top-scoring with an unbeaten 83. He hit the highest score of his first-class career, 154, in the match against Worcestershire, as he and Cyril Smart added 263 for the fourth wicket, to establish a new Glamorgan record.

George Lavis coaching.

In 1935, a strong Sussex team came to Cardiff for the first match of the season and were beaten by three wickets. Sussex scored 288, but Glamorgan replied with 310 – George Lavis top-scoring with 84. Sussex reached 232 in the second innings, but the Welsh county sneaked home with five minutes of extra-time remaining. In the return match at Hastings, Glamorgan had another surprising victory to complete the 'double'. The Welsh side was left to score 165 runs to win in 105 minutes – the runs were made with the game in its last over – George Lavis scoring the lion's share with an unbeaten 65. Against Northamptonshire at Llanelli, after the visitors had been bowled out for 137, Glamorgan scored 349 with Lavis hitting a fine innings of 101 – the first Glamorgan century of the season – his hundred being reached with the last man at the wicket. Glamorgan went on to win by an innings and 109 runs.

During the war, George Lavis served as an officer in the R.A.F. Regiment and showed that he was in good form in the match with an Army XI led by T. N. Pearce at Cardiff, by scoring 116 not out, sharing in two good partnerships with Haines and Smart. After this and other useful wartime performances, he was re-engaged for the 1946 season.

The summer of 1947 was one of his best, as he scored 679 runs at 26.11, his top score being an unbeaten 91 in the victory over Essex.

At the end of that season, the Glamorgan committee were heartened by the improved coaching facilities – George Lavis was appointed coaching organiser to schools and clubs. Through the money raised by the Nursery and Development Fund, he was able to undertake coaching in an indoor school along one of the corridors of the North Stand at the Arms Park, attended by quite a few promising young players, allowing him to groom them for second team appearances.

Though he continued to play occasionally for the first team until 1949, he showed the same enthusiams and zest as he did on the field of play in his new appointment. He had the right disposition for the difficult job of coach – a pleasant manner in the lecture room and a friendly approach to all.

It was George Lavis, who, on seeing the tall, flowing bowling action of Jim McConnon, believed that his future lay as a spinner and during the winter sessions, the astute coach transformed him into a very successful off-spinner.

On 29th July 1956 at Pontypool, George Lavis died after a short illness – the Club had lost their highly rated coach and the person who had guided the development of many of the youngsters in the first team. J. B. G. Thomas summed up the situation by writing: 'Throughout South Wales and Monmouthshire, young players will feel deeply the loss of a kindly tutor and a helpful adviser. In all my travels, I have never met a more sensitive or kinder sportsman.'

TONY LEWIS

Born: 6th July, 1938. Swansea
Played: 1955-1974

FIRST-CLASS GLAMORGAN RECORD

Innings	Not Out	Runs	H.Sc.	Average	100's
546	52	15003	223	30.37	21

Overs	Mdns	Runs	Wkts	Average	Best
55.1	3	306	4	76.50	3-18

NOTABLE FEATS

- He scored 1,000 runs in a season for Glamorgan on 9 occasions.
- He scored 223 v. Kent at Gravesend in 1966.
- In 1966, he set a new Glamorgan record, achieving 2,000 runs by 25th August, the earliest date.
- This was also his best season, when he scored 2,052 runs at 41.87.
- On 20th December 1972, he became the first Glamorgan player to captain England in Test cricket.

SIR NEVILLE CARDUS believed that music and cricket went hand in hand and put his beliefs into practice during a life devoted to both interests. He must have been well-disposed towards Antony Robert Lewis, for like so many youngsters in South Wales, he soon developed an interest in sport and emerged as a talented rugby player and cricketer at Neath Grammar School. He also showed great promise as a violinist and was preparing to go on the Welsh National Youth Orchestra's summer tour in 1955 when he was called up to make his County debut for Glamorgan – it was against Leicestershire, Tony was out for 0, l.b.w. shouldering arms to a vast chinaman from Jack Walsh!

Five years later after his National Service, he entered Christ's College, Cambridge, to win his 'Blue' at cricket and rugby football, and set his feet upon the path to success taken by former Glamorgan captains, Maurice Turnbull and Wilf Wooller, who excelled at both games. In the Varsity match of 1960, he scored 24 and 95 and proved himself a 'master of the cover drive and lofted off-drive', and was unlucky not to get his century. Sir Leonard Hutton emerged from retirement to play for Colonel L. C. Steven's XI in that season and came back from the match saying he had seen a batsman who 'will make a good one'. In his first year at Cambridge, he headed the batting with 1,307 runs and an average of 43.56. In his second year, he was honorary secretary, but was troubled with a persistent knee injury that kept him out of many matches and virtually put an end to his rugby career – he had played full-back for Gloucester and Neath, as well as Cambridge. His batting fell away, but as captain in 1962, he recovered his form and once again headed the batting averages with 1,365 runs and a higher average.

He achieved a personal ambition by scoring a century in the 1962 Varsity match, thus emulating a former Glamorgan 'Blue', J. T. Morgan.

On coming down from Cambridge, he became a permanent member of the Glamorgan side under the captaincy of Ossie Wheatley and he began his long period of readjustment from University cricket and the delights of Fenner's, to the varying wickets of county cricket and especially those of Glamorgan. At Hastings though, he shared the then Glamorgan second wicket record with a partnership of 238 with Alan Jones in the match against Sussex.

Lewis perservered through bad times and good, as the critics attacked and some said he would never make it. For Glamorgan, he scored 1,211 runs in 1963; 1,199 in 1964; and 1,072 in 1965, before blossoming forth in 1966 with 2,198 runs in all matches at 41.47, just failing to beat Parkhouse's record. He hit five centuries, including one at Neath and the 'local lad' had proved himself. It was also the season when he hit his career best score of 223 against Kent at Gravesend.

At the end of the season, he was appointed captain, taking over the reins from Wheatley as leader for 1967. Two seasons later, he was leading the team to the County Championship for only the second time in the Club's history. His team had won several awards from national newspapers and they stored up the crates of champagne for the Championship-winning party on the evening of the victory over Worcestershire.

The County's success was based upon the excellent team spirit which Lewis as captain had forged and that everyone made an important contribution at one time or another. At the end of the season, Tony went to a host of functions to celebrate their win. In fact, the story goes that so often did he make a speech during the autumn months that when his young daughter banged with her spoon on the table at home, he automatically rose to say a few words!

At the end of the 1969 season, Lewis was appointed captain of M.C.C.'s touring team to the Far East. His appointment to captain the near-England strength team against Pakistan indicated that interest remained favourable at Lord's. A century for Glamorgan and then a score of 87 – when he might have scored a second hundred if he hadn't been batting for a declaration – were preliminary to top score in the first M.C.C. innings against the Pakistanis and an enterprising declaration.

On 20th December 1972, Tony Lewis became the first Glamorgan player to captain England in Test cricket by leading out the team for the first Test at the Feroz Shah Kotla ground in Delhi. He made an inauspicious start with a duck, going leg-before to Chandrasekhar. In the second innings, he shared in an unbeaten partnership of 101 with Tony Greig for the fifth wicket to steer England to a six-wicket victory shortly after lunch on Christmas Day. Lewis scored 70 not out and described it as the innings that gave him the greatest pleasure. It was England's first victory in Delhi and their first victory in India since 1951-52. In the fourth Test at Kanpur, he scored his maiden Test century, making 125 in brilliant style – it was the first Test century scored by an England player since Brian Luckhurst's, also against India, eighteen months earlier.

Tony's qualities as a batsman lay in his timing, balance, speed of sight, reaction and movement. He drove the ball in a classical manner through the covers and cut with the minimum of risk. His speed was such that he would often set out as if to drive a spinner, sway back without hurry and cut him; or a ball that had swung late into his pads, he would whip away to the boundary.

He had scores of 74 and 88 during the three drawn Tests in Pakistan, but failed in the first home Test against New Zealand in 1973, and appeared in no further Test matches.

By the middle of the 1974 season, he could no longer manage the day-to-day demands of county cricket and decided to retire at the end of the season, in order to broaden his journalistic involvement.

Chairman of Glamorgan, his talents have happily kept him within the first-class game as cricket correspondent of the *Sunday Telegraph*, author of 'Double Century' an outstanding bicentenary history of M.C.C. and more recently T.V. commentator and presenter with the B.B.C.

JIM McCONNON

Born: 21st June, 1922.
Burnopfield, Durham
Played: 1950-1961

FIRST-CLASS GLAMORGAN RECORD

Innings	Not Out	Runs
350	38	4514
H.Sc.	Average	100's
95	14.70	–

Overs	Mdns	Runs	Wkts	Average	Best
5913.2	1593	15656	799	19.59	8-36

NOTABLE FEATS
- He performed the hat-trick v. South Africa at Swansea in 1951.
- He took 100 wickets in a season for Glamorgan on 3 occasions with a best of 136 at 16.17 runs each in 1951.
- He scored 28 off one over from N. Thomson of Sussex at the Arms Park in 1955.
- In 1958, he bowled 12 maiden overs in succession v. Derbyshire at the Arms Park.

IT WAS DURING THE winter of 1949-50 that the County acquired the services of Jim McConnon, a 27-year-old from Durham.

He had played football for Aston Villa, but a bad knee injury had ruined his league career and he moved to South Wales to play for Lovell's Athletic. He also joined Newport Cricket Club, where he began to show promise as a batsman and fast bowler and so the club officials sent him to the Glamorgan Indoor School for further coaching. Harry Jarrett became impressed with his talents, not as a bowler, but as a batsman. George Lavis, the Glamorgan coach, went to have a look at him and it was as the result of some big scores that he eventually joined the Glamorgan staff. The success which McConnon subsequently achieved as a bowler can be attributed to the astute cricket brain of Wilf Wooller, who persuaded him to bowl off-breaks – Lavis, too, believed McConnon was the ideal replacement for Clay and during the winter sessions, the coach transformed him into an useful off-spinner – it became one of the most successful quick change acts in cricket.

In 1951, his first full season, he took 136 wickets at 16.17 each, which placed him high in the list of the national bowling averages. Jim McConnon was one of the heroes of the great victory against South Africa. Glamorgan beat the tourists by 64 runs after South Africa collapsed to 83 all out. Striking a deadly length and spinning the ball viciously, he had figures of six for 27. In one spell, he captured five wickets for 6 runs, including the hat-trick and his figures after tea were six for 10. This was his big day, but he had many other notable feats to his credit – 14 wickets in the match against Derbyshire and 11 against Worcestershire.

A tall, lean, right-arm off-break bowler, his high action and long fingers were ideal for his craft, but he sometimes struggled with his temperament and needed encouragement and careful handling. His best figures with the ball were eight for 36 against Nottinghamshire at Trent Bridge in 1953. He visited India with a Commonwealth side in 1953-54, but was most surprisingly preferred to Jim Laker on Len Hutton's tour of Australia, the following winter (yet injuries compelled his premature return from both expedition).

In 1954-55, he didn't play in any of the Tests, suffering early in the tour with a couple of muscle strains, but getting himself fit again shortly after Christmas. But then at Hobart, he broke the little finger in his right hand whilst stopping a fierce drive from the left-handed Neil Harvey. On seeing the specialist, he was informed that he wouldn't be fit until the end of the tour and so opted to return home. He must have rued his luck in foreign countries, for as I have said, he returned home early the previous winter with a leg injury.

He began his Test career in the match against Pakistan at Old Trafford in 1954 with a spell of three for 12 in six overs and by holding four outstanding catches.

In 1955, he broke a bone in his left hand after falling heavily in the field in the match against Essex at Pontypridd. Forced to sit on the sidelines again, he decided to go into business in Lancashire and play as professional for Burnley. He helped them win the Lancashire League, taking 52 wickets at an average of 6.8.

His success in Lancashire brought great interest from other counties, notably Warwickshire, but Glamorgan had retained his registration. The Welsh County offered him a new contract and the guarantee of a benefit. Accepting these terms, McConnon bowled well in the summer of 1956, taking 99 wickets as he formed a fine partnership with Don Shepherd.

In 1959, he took over a hundred wickets for the third time, and was instrumental in many of Glamorgan's wins – his best figures being eight for 62 against Worcestershire at Swansea.

Playing his last game for the County in 1961, he then spent three seasons with Cheshire before becoming a coach at Stonyhurst College.

Hailing from the same Durham village as Colin Milburn, when he retired from playing cricket he worked with Brian Statham as a Guinness salesman!

MAJID KHAN

Born: 28th August, 1946. Ludhiana, India
Played: 1968-1976

FIRST-CLASS GLAMORGAN RECORD

Innings	Not Out	Runs	H.Sc.	Average	100's
270	17	9610	204	37.98	21

Overs	Mdns	Runs	Wkts	Average	Best
723.3	216	1674	51	32.82	4-48

NOTABLE FEATS
- He scored a hundred before lunch on three occasions: 147 v. West Indies at Swansea in 1969; 114* v. Worcestershire at Sophia Gardens in 1969 and 113 v. Warwickshire at Edgbaston in 1972.
- He peformed the hat-trick v. Oxford University at Oxford in 1969.

MAJID KHAN

- He took five for 24 in the 1969 Gillette Cup match v. Northamptonshire at Northampton.
- He scored 100* in 70 minutes v. Warwickshire at Edgbaston in 1972.
- He scored 204 v. Surrey at the Oval in 1972.
- He scored 1,000 runs in a season for Glamorgan on 5 occasions, with his best season being 1972 when he scored 1,332 runs in all first-class matches at 66.60, including six centuries.

M AJID KHAN was born to cricket – his father Dr Jahangir Khan, formerly Director of Education for the Government of West Pakistan and a lecturer in history at Punjab University, was a pace bowler, Cambridge Blue and Indian Test player; his brother Asad, also a Cambridge Blue, while his cousins, Imran Khan and Javed Burki both captained Pakistan.

Majid played for Lahore, although he was born in India at Ludhiana in 1964, but in the partition of 1947, his parents had moved to Pakistan and here at St Anthony's High School, he was soon regarded as a youngster of considerable ability. No doubt the influence of his father became obvious during Majid's development and by the time he joined Aitchison College he was recognised as an intelligent young bowler who could also bat. His initial appearance in first-class cricket, at the age of fifteen for Lahore, was quite surprising, when he scored 111 not out and followed this by taking six for 67 on a hard and lifeless wicket against Khairpur Division. It was a remarkable peformance which gained him selection for the Eaglets team which toured England in 1963. In the first-class games on this tour, he bowled economically to head the averages, taking his wickets with fast medium bowling for a little over 11 runs each. Averaging 25 with the bat, he was obviously a good prospect for the full Pakistan Test team and he undoubtedly benefited from playing in a good standard of cricket through the summer.

Two years later, he entered Punjab University reading History and Political Science, and it was while he was in University that he showed how he could completely dominate a game and change its course. Batting in the Ayub Trophy match, Karachi Division had left Punjabs to score 370 to win, but the University had already lost four wickets with just 5 runs on the board, when Majid went to the crease. Immediately another wicket fell without addition to the score, then Majid took the game under control, dictating play with a dynamic display of batting to score 286 not out and see Punjab home to a one wicket win.

He first played Test cricket at the age of 18 years 26 days as a pace bowler – he dismissed Bill Lawry twice, and Booth all with bouncers in his first Test – it was a really nasty delivery, quick and coming straight at the eyes. But, after his action was questioned, he turned in the main, to batting.

Touring England with Pakistan in 1967, he failed miserably in the Test matches, but exploded into a tornado of batting fury when the tourists played Glamorgan at Swansea. Most of the first two days had been slow then on the third day, Majid batting at No. 5, said that he would score a fast hundred as he left the pavilion. It may have been confidence in himself, or a day that comes just once in a while when everything goes well and he rode his luck for 147 not out in eighty-nine minutes before lunch, collecting a century in sixty-one minutes on the way. Roger Davis, the young Glamorgan spinner, was savaged for five sixes in one over as Majid and Saeed Ahmed put on 215 in eighty-five minutes. It came as no real surprise then that Glamorgan offered him a three-year contract and hoped that he could do for them what he could achieve against them. Before joining Glamorgan he had hoped to get a degree from Punjab but postponement of the examination until May caused him to miss them. Political unrest in Pakistan closed the universities for several months in 1969, and again he was unable to sit, but in October 1969, he entered Emmanuel College, Cambridge, to complete his degree course. At Cambridge, he bridged the gap between the Test players and the rest of the side by means of encouragement, coaching and superb captaincy on the field, leading them to their first win over Oxford for fourteen years.

In 1968, he hit over 1,300 runs for Glamorgan and helped the side to a number of victories. His best innings was an 85 he made against Surrey on a difficult Neath wicket, on which no other batsman of either side made fifty. The following season, Majid played a brilliant innings of 156 not out against Worcestershire at Sophia Gardens out of a Glamorgan total of 256. He produced a marvellous range of brilliant strokes on a pitch that was dry and breaking up and against an excellent attack. It was one of several superb 'knocks' from Majid for Glamorgan that season and his accumulation of 1,547 runs played a major part in the County Championship triumph.

Majid believed that the ball should be met with the shot that it merits. He was so relaxed as a player that he seemed to dig the ball out later than most thus creating an impression of being basically a bottom-handed player. But his top hand was certainly in control when on the front foot! In 1974, he reached a century inside 28 overs for Pakistan against England in a one-day international at Trent Bridge. The following year he hit 213 as he and Shafiq Ahmed put on a record 389 for Punjab's first wicket against Sind. Later that year in a John Player League match at Wellingborough he made 75 in twenty-seven minutes.

He was appointed captain of Glamorgan in 1973 and gave many hours of delight to the cricketing public of Wales, but in 1976 as the team struggled, there was growing criticism of Majid's captaincy. There had been talk over the last couple of seasons in some quarters about dissatisfaction over the Pakistani's style of leadership. Sadly, he became more and more isolated from the team as the criticism of his leadership mounted.

A proud and sensitive man, he asked to be omitted from the team to play Somerset at Weston-super-Mare and quit the county scene amidst widespread public confusion.

After leaving Glamorgan, he went to Australia to play for Queensland, where he made two centuries before appearing to lose interest. In October 1976, be became one of the few batsmen to score a century before lunch on the first morning of a Test match, against New Zealand, at Karachi. A deceptively good off-spinner, his apparently innocuous offerings brought the downfall of Boycott, Gower and Botham in the World Cup quarter-final at Headingley in 1979.

Despite his brilliance, it must be doubted if Majid quite realised his full potential – yet on the other hand, he made many good friends on the international cricketing circuit.

AUSTIN MATTHEWS

Born: 3rd May, 1904. Penarth
Died: 29th July, 1977
Played: 1937-1949

FIRST-CLASS GLAMORGAN RECORD

Innings	Not Out	Runs
71	24	691
H.Sc.	Average	100's
37	14.70	0

Overs	Mdns	Runs	Wkts	Average	Best
1473.1	352	3607	227	15.88	7-57

NOTABLE FEATS
- In 1937 he topped the national first-class bowling averages with 45 wickets at 13.66.
- The following year, he topped Glamorgan's bowling averages with 30 wickets at 13.16.

GLAMORGAN WERE POORLY organised in the 1920s and they let this Penarth-born, St David's Lampeter educated Welshman slip through their net to Northampton, where he played for eight seasons, but was never happy with his lot. At that time, he was merely a useful member of one of the weakest county sides on the circuit – in fact, his performances would not have gained him a place in a leading county side. He made two centuries, whilst his 567 wickets had cost him 26.45 runs each.

In 1937, he went to coach rugby at Stowe School and threw in his lot with Glamorgan, making his first appearance at the end of July. He proved a great asset to the Welsh side in the latter half of that season, taking 45 wickets at 13.66. In little more than two weeks, his bowling had created such an impression, especially at Hastings where, on a perfect wicket, he took 14 for 132, and he was subsequently picked for England in the final Test against New Zealand at the Oval, thereby becoming the first Glamorgan professional to play in Tests. Here, on an unresponsive pitch, he bowled respectably and by no means disgraced himself. In what proved to be his only appearance for England, Matthews took the wicket of opener Walter Hadlee in both innings. In the county match against the tourists at Cardiff, he rocked the opposition with a fiery opening spell to take three cheap wickets.

He returned after the war and six lost seasons, having served as a flight lieutenant, to assist Johnny Clay in the re-grouping and restarting of Glamorgan cricket in 1946, but the following year he returned to Stowe School, which he later left for a business appointment in the Eastern Counties.

His best season was 1946 when he took 88 wickets at 14.03 runs apiece. Againt Sussex at Horsham, he demolished the opposition with a personal tally of six wickets for 13 runs as Sussex were bowled out for 33. A typical sample of his bowling occured at Pontypridd in the match against Somerset, which was ruined by rain. However, the two captains, Clay and Barnwell, arranged 'freak' declarations. This ritual being completed, Matthews took seven Somerset wickets for 12 runs, bowling to a ring of eight fielders within a few yards of the bat, as Somerset were dismissed for 53. In fact, he had a spell of seven for 3 in 38 balls! He also returned the inexpensive figures of:

O.	M.	R.	W.
27	16	18	3

in the match against Nottinghamshire at Ebbw Vale. A wonderfully consistent bowler in length and direction, the close-in fielders never had a moment's unease.

An exceptional all-round sportsman, he was a Welsh table tennis international and a rugby trialist – playing for Northampton and East Midlands as well as his native Penarth – he was most unlucky not to be recognised by the parochial Welsh selectors.

His forthright views on coaching were imparted to Cambridge University players from 1930 to 1950, duties he combined with those at Stowe, and in Wisden 1966, he wrote 'Cricket a Game – Not a Subject'.

Spread over five seasons on either side of the war, he took 225 wickets for Glamorgan at the astonishingly low cost of 15.88 runs apiece. A tall man, standing well over 6ft, he was strong, upright and looked indestructable. He bowled fast-medium with a high action, having the ability of keeping the ball on the wicket and making it run away.

In his day, Austin Matthews was a model of fast-medium efficiency as a bowler, taking 816 wickets at 23.40 runs apiece, mostly in a poor side. In his early days, he was a useful slip fielder and a capable batsman with 5,916 runs to his credit, at an average of 16.48.

His death at Penrhyn Bay, North Wales, on 29th July 1977 at the age of 72, came as a great surprise to his many admirers in South Wales. He never seemed to gain the rewards that his ability merited, but as Wilf Wooller wrote in a tribute to the Welsh bowler: 'I personally can pay him no higher tribute as a man of high moral character and as a coach than that my sons should come under the beneficient influence of such a person.'

MATTHEW MAYNARD

Born: 21st March, 1966. Oldham
Played: 1985-

FIRST-CLASS GLAMORGAN RECORD

Innings	Not Out	Runs	H.Sc.	Average	100's
334	33	12603	243	41.87	24

Overs	Mdns	Runs	Wkts	Average	Best
99.0	10	478	5	95.60	3-21

NOTABLE FEATS
- He scored a century on his debut v. Yorkshire at Swansea – the youngest centurion for Glamorgan.
- He is the youngest player to be awarded his Glamorgan cap.

- He scored the fastest ever 50 for Glamorgan in 14 minutes v. Yorkshire.
- He has hit hundreds in all the one-day competitions: 151* v. Durham in the Nat West Trophy; 115* v. Combined Universities in the Benson and Hedges Cup and 101 v. Derbyshire in the Sunday League.
- He scored 243 v. Hampshire at Southampton in 1991.

AS A BATSMAN, Matthew Maynard is an exceptionally talented and exciting middle-order batsman. His upright stance, balanced footwork, cover-driving and straight hitting are from the classical school of batting, yet he was educated at Ysgol John Hughes in Menai Bridge, Anglesey. He was born though in Oldham, where his late father achieved some success in the Lancashire League as a professional for Duckenfield. At the age of seven, Matthew moved with his family to Menai Bridge, where his father took over as licensee of the Liverpool Hotel. Whilst still at school, he represented his county and North Wales and it was quite obvious that the youngster could have a future as a professional cricketer.

In 1982, he joined Kent as a young professional, and though he went on to make several appearances for their 2nd XI and Under-25 team, it really was a frustrating two-and-a-half years batting behind the fast emerging talents of Simon Hinks and Graham Cowdrey. So, when Colin Page, the Kent coach, offered to contact his opposite number, Alan Jones, at Glamorgan to see if they'd be interested in taking him on, it was just the break he'd been looking for.

After scoring a century against Hampshire 2nd XI at Cardiff in 1984, he continued his development under the watchful eye of Alan Jones to become the leading run-scorer in the Glamorgan 2nd XI in 1985 with 753 runs at an average of 41.83. By August of that season, the Glamorgan selectors decided to blood some of their youngsters as the side were out of the reckoning in the County Championship.

Maynard enjoyed a remarkable debut for Glamorgan on August 27th 1985, hitting a superb century against Yorkshire at Swansea, to become the first Glamorgan batsman since Frank Pinch in 1921 to score a hundred in his first Championship innings.

Glamorgan were chasing a target of 272 runs after a series of declarations and as Maynard reached the crease, the Glamorgan score stood on 120 for four. Soon after, a further three wickets fell as the Yorkshire spinners, Carrick and Swallow, extracted spin and bounce from the worn wicket. Maynard then began his lone assault on the Yorkshire attack, advancing time and time again down the wicket to strike some exciting boundaries. After just over an hour at the crease, he reached his 50, but by now the Glamorgan scoreboard read 185 for nine, and the other debutant, slow left-arm bowler, Philip North, was making his way out to the middle. By the time he had got into the eighties, the majority of the spectators believed he would look for the singles, but he hit three successive straight sixes off Phil Carrick to reach a truly amazing century! His 100, made in just 87 minutes, had come off 98 balls and included five sixes and 13 fours. The scoreboard now read 237 for nine and an unbelievable victory looked possible if he could stay at the crease for a few more deliveries, but two balls later, the innings and the match ended, as he was caught at backward point.

Maynard departed to a standing ovation – the youngest person ever to score a first-class century for Glamorgan.

He was without doubt the Welsh side's batting star of 1987. He deservedly won the Apex Packaging Award for the Glamorgan Player of the Year after finishing the season as the side's leading run scorer, with 1,626 runs at an average of 40.65. He hit the headlines with a magnificent century before lunch against Somerset at Weston, going on to make 160, his highest score to date. He followed this the next day with the fastest televised Sunday League fifty against the same attack, though probably his best innings came later in the season when he hit the Derbyshire battery of pace bowlers to all parts of the Chesterfield ground.

He began the 1988 season with successive Championship hundreds against Gloucestershire and Somerset, followed by a Benson and Hedges 'Man of the Match' century against the Combined Universities. He gave a remarkable batting performance against Nottinghamshire in the quarter-final of the Benson and Hedges Cup. A week before he had chipped a bone in his left index finger and was doubtful for the match right up until the very morning of the game. He arrived at the crease with Glamorgan on 32 for two, chasing 221. Launching into a savage assault on the Notts bowlers, he made 107 off just 117 balls to see the Welsh county into the semi-finals of the competition for the first time ever. Luck wasn't with him in the semi-final as Glamorgan chased 218 against Derbyshire. Facing the searing pace of Michael Holding, he knocked off his strapless helmet with his left forearm – the falling helmet knocking off a bail. It was a season in which he played many attacking and outstanding innings for Glamorgan and was chosen by the Test selectors for England's final encounter that summer with the West Indies. His baptism was ill-timed, for it appeared that no-one had told him he was playing in a five-day Test match! Looking extremely nervous during a maiden innings lasting only six balls, he survived decapitation by a Marshall bouncer, a close run-out appeal and being dropped at short leg. He raised all our hopes with a superb cover-drive before finally succumbing to an attempted slash off a bouncer well outside his off stump.

He won the Cricket Writers' Club 'Cricketer of the Year' award that season. He enjoys watching the game and often listens to James Taylor's music on his personal stereo before he goes in to bat – an indication of his relaxed attitude.

In 1991, he scored 1,766 runs, including a career best of 243 against Hampshire at Southampton, and would more than likely have been involved in the World Cup, but for the ban he incurred for touring South Africa. For the 1992 season, Maynard was promoted to vice-captain. It was a unanimous decision by Butcher, senior coach Alan Jones and second-team coach John Steele, that Maynard, a gifted but erratic player, of whom the best has probably not been seen, should have the chance.

Maynard had an extended early opportunity to prove his worth as Butcher rested a calf injury – and though Hugh Morris had been re-appointed to lead the County in 1993, it was thought Maynard's accession may be brought about quicker than planned and so it has proved.

At the I.C.C.'s annual meeting on 8th July 1992 at Lord's, the motion to lift the five-year bans from the 16 English cricketers who toured South Africa in 1990 was passed without opposition.

It was an eventful season for Maynard, as he was restored to the England Test side along with Steve Watkin. This was the first time that the selectors had deprived the County of two players for the same England team. In 1994, Matthew Maynard, by 25 runs, failed to reach four figures for the first time but rectified the situation in 1995 with 1,569 first-class runs..

Recently appointed County captain, all Glamorgan supporters will be hoping the likeable Lancashire-born batsman can lead the County onto further honours.

JACK MERCER

Born: 22nd April, 1895.
Southwick, Sussex
Died: 31st August, 1987
Played: 1922-1939

FIRST-CLASS GLAMORGAN RECORD

Innings	Not Out	Runs
578	100	5730
H.Sc.	Average	100's
72	11.98	0

Overs	Mdns	Runs	Wkts	Average	Best
13813.5	3242	34058	1460	23.32	10-51

NOTABLE FEATS
- He hit 50 in 30 minutes v. Yorkshire at Bradford in 1924.
- In 1926, he took 129 wickets at 16.15 runs each.
- He caused a sensation in the match v. Warwickshire at Cardiff in 1929 dismissing three batsmen in the first over of the match. He ended the season with 137 wickets at 20.35 runs each.
- He hit 31 in 9 minutes v. Somerset at Cowbridge in 1932, a season in which he also perfomed the hat-trick v Surrey at the Oval.
- In 1936, he took 127 wickets at 19.37 runs each.
- In 1939, he had 93% of the monopoly of the runs scored, 41 out of 44 in ten minutes v. Worcestershire at Cardiff, including 31 off an over from R. Howorth.

No County Club could have a more loyal player than Jack Mercer. Loyalty meant everything to him. It is reflected in his own playing career, for from 1922 (though he didn't start playing for Glamorgan regularly until 1924) he bowled nearly 14,000 overs and took 1,460 wickets for an average of 23.32.

As a young man, he played very little cricket and spent several years in Czarist Russia before returning to England when the First World War broke out.

Having played for Sussex since 1919, where the presence of Maurice Tate limited him to just 12 appearances, he readily joined Glamorgan for the 1922 season for £5 per week. He would bowl the same immaculate length all day. He modelled his style on Maurice Tate, probably through his early associations with Sussex, and for a bowler of his type, his stamina was amazing.

I suppose the secret was his cosy, natural action. Mercer was so beautifully poised and balanced in his run up and delivery, and could keep one end going for hours – as indeed he did on many a tiring day. In 1925, he took 96 wickets, but bettered that the following season with 129 at 16.15 each to finish second to Wilfred Rhodes in the national bowling averages.

Against Worcestershire at Dudley, the home team collapsed and were all out for 98 with Mercer taking seven for 40. Bell then completed the first double-century for Glamorgan, enabling the County to declare at lunch-time on the second day, at 470 for six. Needing 372 to avoid an innings defeat, Worcestershire had no chance and lost by an innings and 88 runs, Mercer taking six for 58, making his match record 13 wickets for 98 runs.

The return match at Cardiff was drawn, with the visitors being very lucky to save the match. Little play was possible on the first two days, the first day being completely blank, but on the Tuesday, good progress was made. Turnbull hit his first century, as he and Mercer added 70 runs in half an hour for the sixth wicket to enable Clay to declare at 272 for five. Interest seemed to be going from the game, but Mercer bowled in devastating style to take six wickets for 33 runs, as Worcestershire were bowled out for 95. Following-on, they were 33 for four, before a stand developed and the match was eventually drawn.

His best figures that season were eight for 39 against Gloucestershire at Swansea, though a thrilling match ended with Glamorgan defeated by eight runs.

At the end of the season, Jack Mercer's ability was recognised by him being selected to tour India with Arthur Gilligan's M.C.C. team, an honour richly deserved by one of the best 'county-class' players in England. He also played for the Players at the Scarborough Festival, but bowled only ten overs without taking a wicket.

In 1929, he caused a sensation in the match against Warwickshire at Cardiff, dismissing three batsmen – Kilner, Bates and R. E. S. Wyatt – in the first over of the match, before he had conceded a run. The South African touring team visited Pontypridd for the Whitsun match, and won by 170 runs, Mercer's fine bowling of 14 for 119 not being sufficient to counteract two batting failures.

He ended the season with 137 wickets at 20.35 – it was marvellous achievement, for at that time, many of the Glamorgan slip fielders reactions were slow and many catches were spilled. He would often bowl endless spells to the opposing batsmen, trying very hard to dismiss them with an unplayable ball. When he did produce a lethal delivery to a batsman of the calibre of Hobbs or Sutcliffe, it would often find a thick edge and lob gently to first or second slip, where it was dropped. 'Bad luck old boy' or 'Well stopped Sir' were the comments uttered by a very patient Jack Mercer, who realised he would have to clean bowl his opponents!

The following summer, he turned in many good performances, with Worcestershire again the county to suffer. At Worcester, he took eight for 41 in the home side's second innings total of 143, while in the return match at Cardiff, he collected match figures of ten for 64, as Glamorgan won by 215 runs.

After carrying the brunt of the bowling for several seasons, Mercer's figures declined, though he was leading wicket-taker in 1933 with 79 at a cost of 30.75. In 1934, he was far below form, but this was due to a certain extent to an injury received early in the season.

Although he made his reputation as a bowler, he was a useful lower-order batsman. His best score was 72, when he dominated a last wicket stand of 120 with G. Lavis against Surrey at the Oval that season, but his most memorable innings was an unbeaten 45 in less than 15 minutes against Worcestershire at Cardiff in 1939, during which he hit R. Howorth for 31 runs in one over, the record for an eight-ball over in English cricket, as Glamorgan were just 11 runs ahead on the last afternoon with the last pair at the wicket. He also hit 31 in nine against Somerset at Cowbridge, while his quickest half-century occupied thirty minutes, and that was against Yorkshire in 1924.

In 1935, he returned to his best form, claiming 109 wickets from over 1,000 overs. At the end of the season, the Glamorgan committee decided that his yeoman service should be rewarded and announced that 1936 would be his Benefit year. The Whitsun Holiday match at Cardiff was against Sir Julian Cahn's XI, the game attendance was poor, but the 'gate' was insured, with the result that Mercer had a satisfactory response. The County's first and only Championship victory came in the match against Leicestershire at Swansea, where the bowling of Mercer was the main factor in the match. His twelve wickets for 123 runs ensured that the visitors were dismissed for 94 and 176.

The highlight of the 1936 season came in the match against Worcestershire (who else?) when Jack Mercer became the first and, so far, only Glamorgan bowler to take all ten wickets in an innings. Bowling unchanged, with perfect length and accuracy, he exploited the damp conditions and had all the Worcestershire batsmen in trouble. That day, the heavy atmosphere helped swing and Mercer made the ball move both ways. But there was one awful moment of suspense when George Lavis juggled with the catch which gave Mercer his tenth wicket. Watching impassively as Lavis raced round to get under it, Mercer said quietly to Jack Newman, 'Jack I'll take six shillings to four he drops it.' It was a close run thing – on both counts – Lavis grabbed it, dropped it, knocked it and nudged it, then finally held it and Jack Mercer had taken 'all 10' in 26 overs for 51 runs.

In 1939, he entered the Army, where he carried on his cricket to such an effect that after ten consecutive weekends away from camp his C.O. met him one morning with the greeting that he once had a subaltern by the name of Mercer and could he be the same man. As I wrote earlier, Mercer had as a boy lived for several years in Russia and his knowledge of the language was to be an advantage at the close of the war when he was commanding a group of Ukranians detailed to remove beach defences which he referred to as the Pevensey Bay Meccano Set. Leaving the Army with the rank of captain, he returned to cricket, becoming Northants scorer and playing for them in one match.

An active member of the Magic Circle, he enjoyed many other pastimes, including horse-racing and is reputed to have read of his selection on the M.C.C. tour of India in 1926-27 whilst at the Longchamp Races! A genuine cricketing humourist he was the first Glamorgan player to be a Wisden's Cricketer of the Year.

HUGH MORRIS

Born: 5th October, 1963. Cardiff
Played: 1981-

FIRST-CLASS GLAMORGAN RECORD

Innings	Not Out	Runs	H.Sc.	Average	100's
414	42	14370	166*	38.62	37

Overs	Mdns	Runs	Wkts	Average	Best
58.0	6	380	2	190.00	1-6

NOTABLE FEATS
- He has scored 1,000 runs in a season for Glamorgan on 5 occasions, with a best of 2,276 runs in 1990, including 10 hundreds – both Glamorgan records.
- In 1987, he scored 115 and 105 v. Warwickshire at Edgbaston.
- He shared in Glamorgan's record stand of 249 with S. P. James for the 2nd wicket v. Oxford University in 1987.
- He has scored hundreds in all-day competitions, with bests of: 154* v. Staffordshire at Cardiff in the Nat West Trophy, 143* v. Hampshire at Southampton in the Benson and Hedges Cup and 100 . Derbyshire at Ebbw Vale in the Sunday League.

THERE IS A SCHOOL of thought that Glamorgan should be led by a Welshman in order to preserve the identity of the County, and it is argued that the team has in fact, been most successful with a Welshman in charge! Born in Cardiff, Hugh Morris first came to the attention of Glamorgan's talent scouts when he set a host of records whilst at Blundell's and between 1978 and 1981, he amassed over 2,300 runs for the school's 1st XI. His schoolboy career culminated in 1981, with 923 runs for Blundell's at an average of 184.60, to win him Gray-Nicholls 'Most Promising Schoolboy' Award. In 1982, he amassed 1,032 runs at an average of 149.20, and was selected to play for Young England against Young West Indies and in the following season, led Young England against their counterparts in Australia.

– *Famous Cricketers of Glamorgan* –

HUGH MORRIS

He made his debut for Glamorgan's 2nd XI as a 17-year-old in 1980. Following a further string of good innings for the second team in 1981, including 103* against Warwickshire, Hugh made his first-class debut against Leicestershire at the end of the season.

His subseqent first-team appearances were restricted by his studies for a Physical Education degree at the South Glamorgan Institute of Higher Education, but the brief glimpses the Welsh side's supporters had of the left-hander left them in no doubt that he would in the years ahead play a major role in Glamorgan cricket.

He played many attractive innings in the middle order over the next couple of seasons and his maiden first-class hundred, 114*, eventually came in the match against Yorkshire at Cardiff in 1984.

He took over the Glamorgan captaincy in July 1986, and at 22 years of age became the Club's youngest ever captain. His side was bottom of the Championship table, without any wins and were out of contention for any of the one-day honours. In fact, in his first game in charge, he led the County to victory against Leicestershire and then the following weekend hit his first century in the Sunday League at Ebbw Vale in the match against Derbyshire. It was during 1986 that his winter coaching and playing in Pretoria paid dividends. He showed a much more positive and confident approach, recording eight fifties and a career best 128* against Kent at Maidstone.

A few considered at the time that Hugh's relative inexperience at county level might count against him, but as Secretary Philip Carling pointed out 'the fact that he is one of the youngest captains of all time is a great tribute to his maturity'. Of course, Hugh possessed a considerable amount of experience of captaincy, having led English Schools, Young England and was both cricket and rugby captain at Blundell's School. The captaincy didn't affect his game that summer; indeed he celebrated his promotion in the Northamptonshire match at Swansea by scoring 90 and 88.

Hugh Morris was elevated to the captaincy as part of a long-term strategy aimed at bringing much needed stability to the Club – for he was the ninth county captain in only 10 years. However, his own game slipped while he tried to look after others in the team and so midway through the 1989 season, he handed over the reins to Alan Butcher (born in Croydon!)

During the winter months, he worked hard at rectifying a few minor faults in his technique. He eliminated a tendency that he had to chase deliveries slanted across him, used a lighter bat and adjusted his grip, so that he now played with a much more straight bat.

On the opening day of the 1990 sesaon, he hit a hundred against Oxford University and at the end of May, a sparkling century followed against the powerful Worcestershire attack in the Benson and Hedges Cup quarter-final. He was bitterly disappointed not to have been among the 43 names that were announced in July of that year in England's short list for the winter tours. In fact, he was so upset that he vented his anger by scoring five hundreds in his next nine County Championship matches, including a career best 160 against Devon Malcolm and Derbyshire at Sophia Gardens. It was an innings of the highest order, full of shots against a team with a renowned attack – the next highest score was 31. Other England bowlers suffered as Hugh hit a century off Middlesex's Cowans, Fraser, Williams and Emburey, and two off a Worcestershire side that contained Dilley, Botham and Newport. He hit hundreds in each innings, 110 and 102* in the match against Nottinghamshire at Worksop, and in August, there was a concerted campaign by the media, pressing Morris's claim for a place in the Australian tour party. Even Alan Jones added his weight, saying, 'I'm a firm believer in picking players in form, and on this basis, Hugh Morris has to go. He's been the most consistent batsman in the country this season.'

A record 10 centuries for Glamorgan that summer earned Morris a Championship average of 51.72 and an invitation from the England Selection Committee to captain the England 'A' team to Sri Lanka in the New Year. The overjoyed Morris said, 'I gave up the Glamorgan captaincy to try to gain an England place, so I'm delighted with the news.' Though he had a disappointing tour, he returned to South Wales and began to find his form again.

On 25th July 1991, he made his Test debut for England in the fourth Test against the West Indies at Edgbaston. He was unfortunate to touch a ball angled across him in the second over by Patterson – it was a cruel personal blow for a player who has not known whether he has been coming or going as an England prospect, only to be chosen whilst in a lean trot, having just bagged a pair against the same opposition. In the fifth Test he displayed admirable courage and resolution, as he elected to get into line and play the ball instead of evading it. He played some good strokes off both feet through the off-side, but was hit in the face by Ambrose, who soon ended his brave defiance. Against Sri Lanka, he was looking increasingly confident before he was trapped lbw for 42. He ended the summer at the head of the Glamorgan averages with 1,601 runs at 69.60 and was selected for the England 'A' tour to Bermuda and the West Indies.

When he had led the England 'A' side early in 1991, he was still thought to be a limited captain, possibly through limited self-belief. But in 1991-92 when the 'A' team job returned to him following injury to Martyn Moxon, he was by all accounts, a revelation. He returned ready to take on the Glamorgan job again, whenever Alan Butcher may decide to retire. When Hugh Morris resigned the captaincy, the County committee were very understanding and there was an spoken understanding that Morris might at some future date, return to the post.

Yet, just two days before the start of the 1992 season, he was informed by Alan Butcher, that he no longer held any position of responsibility. However, he was restored to the Glamorgan captaincy for the 1993 season and was at the forefront of the County's revitalisation and the burden of captaincy has if anything enhanced his batting. He was the first to reach a thousand first-class runs and continued in good form in all competitions.

After leading the England 'A' side to South Africa, he had a disappointing season in 1994, averaging only 28 in the Championship and failing to make 1,000 runs for the first time since 1988. Worse still, his benefit season ended with hospital surgery on a left knee damaged severely enough to raise doubts about his future.

Hugh Morris is only 31 and ought logically to have years ahead of him in the game but after three operations on his right knee, the collapse of his previously sound one is worrying.

Having relinquished the captaincy at the end of the 1995 season, the County certainly need him back as a batsman and at his best.

LEN MUNCER

Born: 23rd October, 1913. Hampstead
Died: 18th January, 1982
Played: 1947-1954

FIRST-CLASS GLAMORGAN RECORD

Innings	Not Out	Runs	H.Sc.	Average	100's
333	46	6460	135	22.50	4

Overs	Mdns	Runs	Wkts	Average	Best
6642.2	1807	14462	708	20.42	9-62

NOTABLE FEATS
- He took nine for 97 v. Surrey at the Arms Park in 1947.
- He took nine for 62 v. Essex at Brentwood in 1948.
- He reached 100 wickets in 1948 on 9th July, the second fastest-ever by a Glamorgan player.
- In 1948, he took 156 wickets at 17.12 runs each.
- Against Sussex at Swansea that season, he bowled 545 balls – the most sent down by a Glamorgan player.
- He took 100 wickets in a season for Glamorgan on four occasions.
- In 1951, he scored 107* and took 10 for 57 in the match v. Derbyshire at Chesterfield.
- He did the 'double' in 1952, with 1,076 runs at 24.45 and 100 wickets at 17.53 runs each.
- He shares the Glamorgan sixth-wicket record partnership of 230 with Willie Jones v. Worcestershire at Worcester in 1953.

A VERY CAPABLE ALL-ROUNDER, Len Muncer joined the Lord's groundstaff in 1929. He played his first game for Middlesex in 1933, at the age of 19, as a batsman and leg-spin bowler. If there was one department in which Middlesex had a surfeit, it was in leg-spinning all-rounders. Jim Sims, R. W. V. Robins, H. G. Owen-Smith and J. H. Human all answered to this description, while Ian Peebles was superior to them all.

Len Muncer, 1947-54, off-spinner and batsman – a valuable acquisition from Middlesex.

He could not quite hold his place in a strong Middlesex side, and by the time war came, several highly-talented contemporaries, headed by the names of Compton, Edrich, Brown and Robertson, had overtaken him as a batsman and as Len, taken prisoner at Singapore in the Second World War, looked ahead from the jungle camps on the Burma-Siam railway, his future must have seemed dreams away!

In 1946, he returned to Lord's not yet wholly fit again and did very little, but in 1947, he was taken on by Glamorgan on a special registration, where be blossomed as a talented all-rounder.

His 82 matches for Middlesex brought him the moderate return of 1,944 runs at 17.67 and 23 wickets at 28.17 with 24 catches.

He soon won his County cap for his accurate off-break bowling and – now his second string – his sound and resolute right-hand batting; he was also a very good slip fielder. It was under Wilf Wooller's guidance and with the example of that old master of the art, Johnny Clay (who in his 50th year still topped the bowling averages) that Muncer turned with such success to off-spin, that he took 1,087 wickets at 18.55 runs each, in his first Welsh summer. He had the gifts of flight, length and spin and had the virtue of making the batsman play all six balls of an over. In the match against Surrey at Cardiff, he bowled right through the visitors innings to take nine for 97 after Wooller had taken the first wicket to fall. Glamorgan had little difficulty in winning by four wickets, but Laker gave a few uneasy minutes in the closing stages before victory was finally achieved. A low-scoring match at Cheltenham ended with defeat for the County by 29 runs. After an even first innings, Barnett and Basil Allen opened the Gloucestershire second innings with a stand of 95, only to see Muncer (eight for 36) demolish the rest of the batting in a spell of eight wickets for nine runs, including three wickets in four balls. The game ended when the Welsh side collapsed in the same fashion, with Tom Goddard taking eight for 61.

Then in 1948, came Glamorgan's Championship triumph when the beaming oval-faced spin bowler played a leading role with 156 wickets at 17.12 runs each. He turned in some remarkable bowling performances, including his best of nine for 62 against Essex at Brentwood, when he robbed himself of all ten wickets in an innings by catching the ninth batsman! He took six for 13 on the final day of the match against Nottinghamshire at Swansea, as the visitors were bowled out for 68, chasing 300 to win. Also at Swansea, he took eight for 99, (15 for 201 in the match) his calculated spin being too much for the Sussex batsmen. Reaching his hundredth wicket on 9th July, he was the first in England to reach that target. At one period, some regarded him as the best slow spinner in England and though he never won international honours, he appeared for the Players at Lord's in the 1948 season.

Against South Africa in 1951, he top-scored in Glamorgan's innings of 111 with 30 and continued to thwart the Springboks by taking five for 9, as the tourists slumped to 34 for seven by the tea interval. Eventually, they were also dismissed for 111, before Glamorgan replied with 147 in their second innings. Muncer followed up his first innings seven for 45 with four for 16, as the South African fell 64 runs short. Also that same season, he had a good all-rounder match against Derbyshire at Chesterfield – he scored an unbeaten 107 and had match figures of ten for 57 (five for 34 and five for 23).

In 1952, he had a spell of five for 7 against his former county, Middlesex, as Glamorgan gained their first ever victory at Lord's. It was the season when he performed the 'double' for the only time in his career. He bowled over 800 overs to take in all matches, 105 wickets at 17.29 and amassed 1,097 runs at an average of 24.37, including a career-best 135 against Somerset at Swansea, which justified his promotion up the order to No. 4. The emergence of Jim McConnon, also an off-spinner, restricted his opportunities, and after having been awarded a benefit in 1954, he left the County at the end of the season and returned to Lord's where he eventually became head coach, succeeding W. R. Watkins.

His last first-class match was in 1957, when he played for the M.C.C. against Scotland at Aberdeen. Altogether in 317 matches, he scored 8,646 runs (at 20.88) including four centuries, took 755 wickets (at 20.91) and held 145 catches.

Dying suddenly on January 18th 1982, at the age of 68, his was an unusual cricket career, wherein after initial disappointment, all turned out well in the end.

JACK NASH

Born: 18th September, 1873. Blean, Kent
Died: 6th December, 1956
Played: 1902-1922

FIRST-CLASS GLAMORGAN RECORD

Innings	Not Out	Runs	H.Sc.	Average	100's
225	45	1302	44	7.23	0

Overs	Mdns	Runs	Wkts	Average	Best
4969.3	1567	11872	763	15.56	9-93

NOTABLE FEATS
- He had match figures of 15 for 116 v. Worcestershire at Swansea in 1921.
- He took nine for 93 v. Sussex at Swansea in 1922.

As a bowler, Jack Nash's great virtue was length. He would bowl the natural off-break of the medium right-hander for hours on end – always to a perfect length.

Making his debut for the County in 1902, he was, along with Harry Creber at this stage of the County's history, getting through a great deal of work with little or no support. In his second season, he captured 66 wickets and along with Creber bowled 849 of the 1,056 overs bowled that summer.

Against Surrey II at Cardiff in 1920, there had been no play on the first day, due to heavy rain. When play commenced on the second morning, the visitors were dismissed for 45, with Nash taking four for 8. Glamorgan replied with 139, before dismissing their opponents a second time for just 78, with Nash claiming five for 20, to leave his side the victors by an innings and 16 runs.

He headed the Glamorgan averages in 1921, the season in which the County were awarded first-class status, by taking 91 wickets.

He dismissed 15 Worcestershire batsmen at Swansea at a cost of 116 runs, as the County won by an innings and 53 runs. His tally of 91 wickets was more than twice as many as any other player in the side. His final figures at the end of that season were:

O.	M.	R.	W.	Avr.
695.4	192	1690	91	18.57

He was one of the cricket's unsung heroes, for to take that number of wickets under the conditions that he had to suffer was a remarkable record. Jack Nash was one of the best bowlers of all on a wicket that helped him. His steadiness on good wickets was generally accepted, but whenever the ball was 'doing a bit' there was a vicious bite in Nash's bowling which worried the best of batsmen.

He made his mark in the County's first first-class match against Sussex at Cardiff in May 1921. Glamorgan batted first and totalled a respectable 272. Jack Nash then came along with one of his most hostile spells to take four wickets for 45 in a Sussex total of 152. After Glamorgan had batted for a second time, Sussex needed 334 runs to win. But despite a promising start, Nash and Cooper again got among the wickets to give Glamorgan victory by 23 runs – Nash's figures being six for 131.

He finally retired at the end of the following season, with 133 first-class wickets to his name at a cost of 21.81 runs each. Jack Nash died in a London hospital on 6th December 1956, aged 83.

MALCOLM NASH

Born: 9th May, 1945. Abergavenny
Played: 1966-1983

FIRST-CLASS GLAMORGAN RECORD

Innings	Not Out	Runs	H.Sc.	Average	100's
467	67	7120	130	17.81	2

Overs	Mdns	Runs	Wkts	Average	Best
9193.3	2426	25601	991	25.83	9-56

NOTABLE FEATS

- He took nine for 56 v. Hampshire at Basingstoke in 1975.
- He performed the hat-trick v. Worcestershire at Worcester in a Sunday League game in 1975, finishing with figures of six for 29.
- He scored 115* before lunch v. Surrey at the Oval in 1976
- He holds the Glamorgan record for the most wickets in all three one-day competitions: 215 in the Sunday League, 64 in the Benson and Hedges Cup and 41 in the Gillette/Nat West Trophy.

MALCOLM NASH first came to the attention of Wilf Wooller in the early sixties as a Wells Cathedral School product from an excellent Welsh cricketing stock. His father was prominent in Abergavenny club cricket and his brother was no mean player.

At school, Malcolm opened the bowling, and was a very aggressive No. 3 batsman. He was also a games player of genuine skill and represented Wales at Under-23 level in the game of hockey. Always eager to learn about the game of cricket, he crossed the heads of the valleys to the steel town of Ebbw Vale, where two stalwarts of Somerset cricket, Bill Andrews and Harold Gimblett, imparted their knowledge.

Right from the onset, Nash had a high, easy action, which controlled the direction of the ball, which he could dip in late from the off to middle and leg stumps and which, in the course of time,

– *Famous Cricketers of Glamorgan* –

MALCOLM NASH

was to bring him many an l.b.w. victim! Shortly, this delivery was strengthened by an ability to pitch a ball a little quicker on the seam around the off-stump and move it away to the slip cordon, preventing the batsman lining his shot up too early. It was a development of this technique that enabled him to roll over the best early batsmen in first-class cricket – something he consistently did.

Malcolm made his debut for the Club in 1966, but it was two years later before he established himself, at the age of 23, as a supporting bowler to Ossie Wheatley and Jeff Jones. That season saw Jones, in his prime, break down with an irremediable elbow injury. Malcom Nash stepped into his shoes and never looked back.

That season of 1968 was to prove very eventful for him. His controlled left-arm swing accounted for five Australian wickets as the tourists were bowled out for 110. His figures were:

O.	M.	R.	W.
15.3	6	28	5

including the best ball of the day for Inverarity; it swung into him and, as he made to force it through the onside field, it moved back off the seam and hit the off stump.

Also, at seven minutes past five on Saturday 1st September, he began an over of experimental spin, which he practised occasionally, to Gary Sobers. He was aiming to bring the ball across from off to the left-hander, and was turning the ball enough to be bowling round the wicket. A few minutes later, he became a statistic in Wisden and cricket history for ever. Sobers hit his over for a world-record of six successive sixes. Up to that point, he had been economical and I am assured that it wasn't at all a bad over! Standing defiant among all the hilarity in the dressing room, Nash said: 'One day I will write a book,' to which Tony Cordle enquired: 'What will you call it? Gone with the Wind?'

Nash was awarded his County Cap in the 1969 Championship winning season. He turned in some very telling performances with both bat and ball, and took six for 31, as Gloucestershire were dismissed for 73 on a green wicket at Cheltenham. With his quick eye, he developed an aggressive batting technique. He became an accommodating No. 7 or No. 8 batsman in the Glamorgan side, ending the season with a batting average of 24.60. He would make violent assaults on all forms of opposition bowling when needed, combining the unpredictable with the orthodox, but always relishing his chances!

An exciting batsman, he hit the fastest televised 50 in the John Player League off 33 balls against Kent at Swansea in 1970. He came in when Glamorgan were 57 for seven and when the foreboding voice of Jim Laker was predicting no contest. Glamorgan narrowly won an exciting match with Nash collecting the B.B.C. prize of £250. He set another Glamorgan record by hitting nine sixes in an innings against Gloucestershire, again at Swansea in 1973. Against Surrey in 1976, he hit a century off 61 balls before lunch on the second day when Glamorgan had lost six wickets for next to nothing and were in trouble. Also that season, he hit 103 against Hampshire at Swansea in the Benson and Hedges Cup, in just 62 minutes – a record for the fastest hundred in that competition.

In 1975, he headed the County averages with 85 wickets, including 14 in the victory over Hampshire at Basingstoke, with a career best nine for 56 in the first innings. The advent of the John Player League resulted in Malcolm being regarded as one of the most economical and successful one-day bowlers in the game. For in that 1975 season, he also returned his best figures in the Sunday League, taking six for 29 against Worcestershire, including five wickets in his last seven balls!

I particularly remember Malcolm turning in two very economical bowling analyses against Lancashire in the same competition:

	O.	M.	R.	W.
1979 at Cardiff	8	4	8	1
1980 at Manchester	8	4	8	2

In the Gillette Cup Final of 1977, he dismissed Middlesex and England captain, Mike Brearley, with the first ball of the innings, by drifting the ball across him to have him caught behind. In 1978, he hit Denis Breakwell of Somerset for four consecutive sixes from the first four balls of an over – almost a hint of history in the making, but that was where it ended!

Malcolm captained the County in the 1980 and 1981 seasons. A fair man with a sense of humour, he put forward the view that visiting captains should always win the toss in order to nullify the advantage of pitches, specially prepared for 'home' bowlers – except when Gary Sobers is in your side! Throughout his career, Malcolm Nash took 991 first-class wickets. An analysis of these wickets reveals an exceptionally high strike-rate among the top batsmen. In fact, had he possessed a yard more pace and a little more venom with the old ball, he would have increased his wicket-take among the lower order and almost certainly have represented England.

RODNEY ONTONG

Born: 9th September, 1955. Johannesburg
Played: 1975-1989

FIRST-CLASS GLAMORGAN RECORD

Innings	Not Out	Runs	H.Sc.	Average	100's
413	65	10825	204*	31.10	18

Overs	Mdns	Runs	Wkts	Average	Best
5708.5	1277	17279	531	32.54	8-67

NOTABLE FEATS
- He scored 1,000 runs in a season for Glamorgan on 5 occasions.
- He scored 100 v. Northamptonshire at Abergavenny in the John Player League match of 1982.
- He scored 204* v. Middlesex at Swansea in 1984.
- He had a good all-round match v. Nottinghamshire at Trent Bridge in 1985, scoring 130 and taking 13 for 106.

IT WAS IN 1975 that the Club acquired the services of Rodney Ontong, a 19-year-old all-rounder from South Africa, who had made his debut for Border at the age of 17 years 7 months. He had

– Famous Cricketers of Glamorgan –

RODNEY ONTONG

been on the M.C.C. groundstaff and had played for the Second Eleven on the recommendation of Len Muncer.

By the time the 1977 season got underway, Rodney Ontong was recognised as an English qualified player, following a successful appeal by the Club to the T.C.C.B. that the talented all-rounder had learnt his cricket in this county.

By 1983, he began to show signs of promise as an off-spinner after changing styles from medium-pace. It was during this season that he played a decisive part in shaping a stimulating victory over Surrey at Swansea, scoring 109, with five sixes and 12 fours as the innings gained momentum just when Surrey, oblivious of the danger, thought the home county was digging in for the duration. Glamorgan reached their target of 282 with 22 balls to spare. Ontong also scored two other centuries that season, 112 against Yorkshire at Middlesbrough and 105 not out against Kent at Sophia Gardens. He made some valuable contributions as a bowler, taking six for 64 against Leicestershire at Hinkley and five for 52 against Northants at Northampton, confusing some batsmen with variations of seam, cutters and off-breaks. It was this all-round adaptability that led to him being voted Glamorgan's Player of the Year to earn the Apex Packaging trophy and £500 prize.

He was appointed vice-captain for the 1984 season, and as Mike Selvey resigned midway through the season, he took over in a caretaker capacity for the rest of the season. The change of leadership brought a change of fortune, for Glamorgan won their next two matches. It certainly didn't affect his own form, for in the match against Middlesex at Swansea, he hit the highest score of his career, an unbeaten 204. In fact, it was his best ever season with the bat, as he scored 1,320 runs in the Championship.

A very likeable man, Rodney Ontong took on a very warm seat when he succeeded Mike Selvey and although the side did not win anything, he did a good job and kept the side content.

In 1985, he turned in a remarkable virtuoso performance against Nottinghamshire. Ontong took 13 wickets with his off-breaks, including his best ever figures of eight for 67 – the flightier, more interesting and unusual type of spin – and for good measure, scored 130 to overwhelm Notts by an innings, with just a little help from his friends.

Halfway through the summer of 1986, he began to find the role of captain putting severe pressure on his own game. He decided to step down for the following season, but realised it would benefit his successor if he stood dowm immediately to allow the next captain to gain experience during the second half of the summer.

After he had handed over the captaincy to Hugh Morris, he became a more assertive and impressive player. After missing part of the 1987 season with injury, he decided not to return to his native South Africa for the winter for the first time in 12 years since he first went to Cardiff. Instead, he accepted the chance to play for Western Australia in the Sheffield Shield since Vic Marks, who'd had the job the previous year, was unavailable, though he was hopeful of being part of England's winter tour.

In 1989, the County faced a legal action from their all-rounder, for the injuries received while driving between games late in the 1988 season. This, however, transpired to be an insurance technicality, if a significant one. Ontong, like most county cricketers had third party insurance through his employers, so his initial claim for liability had to be against the Club.

Much of the more serious aspect of the affair was that the injuries effectively ended Rodney Ontong's first-class career – a career which saw him score 14,896 runs and take 823 wickets.

GILBERT PARKHOUSE

Born: 12th October, 1925. Swansea
Played: 1948-1964

FIRST-CLASS GLAMORGAN RECORD

Innings	Not Out	Runs	H.Sc.	Average	100's
759	48	22619	201	31.81	32

Overs	Mdns	Runs	Wkts	Average	Best
37.1	8	125	2	62.50	1-4

NOTABLE FEATS
- In 1950, he scored three centuries in successive innings in first-class matches: 127 v. Combined Services at Cardiff Arms Park and 121 and 148 v. Somerset on the same ground.

- He carried his bat for 60* out of 152 v. Lancashire at Swansea in 1954.
- He holds the Glamorgan record for the earliest date for reaching 1,000 runs in a season on 17th June in both 1950 and 1959.
- He scored 1,000 runs in a season for Glamorgan on 15 occasions.
- He scored 201 v. Kent at Swansea in 1956.
- His best season was 1959, when he scored 2,071 runs at 49.31, including six centuries.
- He holds the Glamorgan record for the fastest hundred, scoring 100* in 70 minutes v. Northants at Northampton in 1961.

HAVING LEARNED HIS cricket at Wycliffe College, Gilbert Parkhouse developed his skills as a stylish opening batsman in wartime matches, but Army duties afterwards delayed his first-class debut until 1948. In his first year, he scored 1,204 runs, while his exceptional catching close to the wicket played no small part in Glamorgan's first Championship success.

In 1950, as one Glamorgan wit put it, 'The team were either watching Parkhouse bat or the rain coming down.' For he had a wonderful run in June and equalled Dai Davies's record by scoring three centuries in successive innings. He passed 1,000 runs on 17th June – the quickest ever for the Welsh County – as he hit a magical 161 out of Glamorgan's total of 448. He hit seven centuries that summer, including hundreds in each innings, 121 and 148 against Somerset at Cardiff. He almost hit another in the match against Surrey when he ran riot by scoring 75 out of 88 in fifty minutes, and was in the running for the fastest century of the year. He was described by some that season as the most gifted batsman to play for the Club. He made 1,997 runs at an average of 45.35 and established a series of new batting records – in fact, he nearly got 1,000 runs in the month of June alone!

The season also saw him called up to play for England in the second Test against the West Indies at Lord's. He was bowled for nought in the first innings by Valentine, but in the second innings, he was most impressive. He showed encouraging confidence and a variety of strokes until he hit a full toss straight to silly mid-off in the last over of the fourth day when wanting only two runs for 50. This mistake came at a time when thoughts were raised that Cyril Washbrook might be capable of saving the match if someone could stay with him. As it was, they were dismissed for 274 to give the West Indies their first victory at Test level in England. He kept his place for the next match at Trent Bridge, where he scored 13 and 69. He missed the last of the four match series through injury, but he had done enough to warrant selection for Freddie Brown's M.C.C. tour of Australia and New Zealand.

He struggled with both illness and injury on the tour and only played in two Tests in Australia, plus one in New Zealand. The high spot of the tour came in the match against New South Wales, where he and Reg Simpson added 228 for the fourth wicket. However, his modest returns at Test level caused the selectors to omit him until 1959.

It had been a disappointing tour for him and he didn't repeat his success of the previous season in 1951, probably due to lapses in timing and concentration.

A typical Parkhouse innings would always contain a series of powerful shots, struck with superb timing and sheer artistry – typified in his career best innings of 201 againt Kent at Swansea in 1956. He exceeded 1,000 runs in a season for the County on fifteen occasions with a best of 2,243 in all matches in 1959.

It was his fine batting that season that brought him back into the Test arena. He scored six centuries and formed a solid opening partnership with Bernard Hedges. He was called up for the third Test against India at Headingley and opened the innings with Lancashire's Geoff Pullar. They shared an opening stand of 146 for the first wicket, at that time, a record. Parkhouse made 78 and kept his place for the next match, where he scored 17 and 49. Unfortunately for Parkhouse, in spite of his fine reputation against pace, the England selectors wanted to give Subba Row a chance in the final Test before naming their squad to tour the Caribbean – Subba Row made 94 and left Parkhouse to muse over the winter months about playing for an unfashionable county! He retired in 1964 with 22,619 runs to his name at an average of 31.81, but he was also an outstanding slip fieldsman, taking 312 catches and became an important member of the County's close to the wicket fielding unit.

He coached Worcestershire in 1966, before accepting a similar appointment at Stewart's and Melville College in Edinburgh.

JIM PRESSDEE

Born: 19th June, 1933. Mumbles
Played: 1949-1965

FIRST-CLASS GLAMORGAN RECORD

Innings	Not Out	Runs	H.Sc.	Average	100's
543	83	13411	150*	29.16	12

Overs	Mdns	Runs	Wkts	Average	Best
3666.2	1095	8988	405	22.18	9-43

NOTABLE FEATS
- He scored two hundreds before lunch: 107* v. Kent at Dartford in 1959 and 102* v. Sussex at the Arms Park in 1961.
- He scored 1,000 runs in a season for Glamorgan on 6 occasions.
- In 1961, he scored 1898 runs at 35.14 and in 1962, 1,911 runs at 34.74.

– *Famous Cricketers of Glamorgan* –

JIM PRESSDEE

- In 1963, he took over 100 wickets in a season for Glamorgan, when he performed the 'double' – 1,435 runs at 34.17 and 104 wickets at 21.04.
- He took nine for 43 v. Yorkshire at Swansea in 1965.

JIM PRESSDEE WAS A forcing right-hand batsman and slow left-arm bowler from the Mumbles area of Swansea.

A Welsh schoolboy soccer international, he was on the staff of Swansea Town Football Club, but at 16 years and 23 days, he became the County's youngest post-war cricketer. Playing in a two-day friendly against the R.A.F. at the Maindy Barracks ground in Cardiff, he took six for 55 from 25 overs, to earn a first-class debut against Nottinghamshire a couple of weeks later during the summer of 1949.

National Service then intervened and he did not play again until 1952, when he rejoined the County staff.

In 1955, his first full season, he topped the County bowling averages with 72 wickets at a cost of 19 runs each and held on to 42 catches in the leg trap. It was a feat that brought him his County cap. His greatest performance that summer came in the match against Middlesex at the Arms Park. On the second day, the home side collapsed against the spin of Fred Titmus and Jack Young on what was a rough, dry wicket and Middlesex were left with just 145 to make for victory. Jim Pressdee slowed them down with some very accurate bowling, but at 110 for five, it still seemed as if the visitors would win inside two days. Then Allan Watkins took two wickets and Wooller claimed the extra half-hour. The captain's faith was justified, as young Pressdee took two further wickets. The final over arrived with Middlesex requiring just six runs to win and Glamorgan one wicket. Jim Pressdee bowled the last over of the day, but after bowling for almost four hours he was unable to take the final wicket. Jack Young took five runs from the over, so stumps were drawn with the scores level. Middlesex won off the third ball of the final day's play, but Jim Pressdee was able to take great pride from his bowling figures, which were:

O.	M.	R.	W.
35	13	47	4

Over the next few years, Jim Pressdee's batting developed to such an extent that in 1959 he was promoted to No. 3. He fully justified this promotion, with his maiden first-class century, and topping the 1,000 run mark for the first time. The following summer, he completely lost form and confidence, scoring less runs and taking only two wickets! By 1963 though, he had rediscovered his bowling ability. It had been suggested that Pressdee's loss of form had been due to overbowling or mishandling by the Club. Whatever the cause of Pressdee's problems, two successive winters of playing club cricket in South Africa allowed him to believe in himself again as a bowler, for he returned to take 104 wickets at 21.04 and thus perform the 'double' for the first time – beginning to prove almost unplayable on the turning wickets of Swansea. When Glamorgan beat the Australians at St Helen's in 1964, Jim Pressdee was in irrepressible form. The Welsh side struggled to reach 197, but a mid-afternoon shower dampened the wicket, to allow 'Pres' and 'Shep' to reduce the tourists to 39 for six. They were dismissed the following day for 101 and then again in their second innings for 232 after Glamorgan had set them 268 to win. Jim Pressdee had match figures of ten for 123 as the Welsh side won by 36 runs.

He had already decided to emigrate to South Africa at the end of the 1965 season, but the way he went left a sour taste in the mouths of many Glamorgan supporters. Glamorgan had just been beaten by Essex at Llanelli inside two days and the County had to settle for third place in the Championship. Emotions were obviously running high at the end of the game as Pressdee tried to leave the pavilion by going through a small back room, where a lot of money and valuables had been left. Secretary, Wilf Wooller, was anxious that the exit be kept closed to prevent any outside pilfering. A heated argument took place, with the result that Jim Pressdee stormed off to the Press tent and told the journalists that one of the reasons for his departure was that he could not get on with the Club Secretary.

All very sad, for in his sixteen years in South Wales, Jim Pressdee scored 13,411 runs and took 405 wickets.

VIV RICHARDS

Born: 7th March, 1952. St John's, Antigua
Played: 1990-1993

FIRST-CLASS GLAMORGAN RECORD

Innings	Not Out	Runs	H.Sc.	Average	100's
82	10	3273	224*	45.45	9

Overs	Mdns	Runs	Wkts	Average	Best
233.0	46	695	9	77.22	3-22

NOTABLE FEATS
- He is the only West Indian to score 100 first-class hundreds.
- Holds the Somerset record individual score, 322 v. Warwickshire at Taunton in 1985.
- He scored 164* for Glamorgan v. Hampshire at Southampton in 1990.
- He has played in 121 Test matches for the West Indies, 50 as captain, scoring 8,540 runs at 50.23, and a highest score of 291 v. England at the Oval in 1976.
- He scored 224* for Glamorgan v Middlesex at Cardiff in 1993.

VIV RICHARDS WAS MORE of a success in Wales than anyone – players and officials included – had dared hope.

Born in the Antiguan capital of St John's on the 7th March 1952, he first played for his native Leeward Islands in the Caribbean's Shell Shield. He joined Somerset in 1974 and spent 13 seasons at Taunton scoring 14,698 runs at 49.82 – his benefit in 1982 raised £56,440. He graduated to the West Indies side in the winter of 1974-75 and was until recently, an automatic selection. In 1976, he scored 1,710 runs in 11 Test matches during the calendar year. He succeeded Clive Lloyd as captain of the West Indies in the spring of 1985, finishing his Test career with 121 appearances and 8,540 runs at 50.23.

It was four years after his much-publicised departure from Somerset, that Viv Richards resumed his county career further

VIV RICHARDS

west with Glamorgan. It had been hoped that Viv would make his Glamorgan debut in 1989, but he missed the whole of that summer through haemorrhoid trouble.

He met up with his new colleagues when Glamorgan's pre-season tour of Trinidad coincided with the Port-of-Spain Test. The Welsh Club felt that he still had the motivation to illuminate county cricket. Disappointed not to play in 1989, he said: 'Wait until 1990, that will be when Glamorgan will see the best of me.'

Viv was true to his word, proving beyond doubt that the signing was no mere gimmick.

The hero arrived just in time – with an escort of armed police officers as he passed through Heathrow Airport – just to add a touch of melodrama on his return to county cricket.

Rumours had been endless over Richards's commitment to the Glamorgan cause.

Some believed that his haemorrhoid trouble would form medical grounds for staying away, while others proposed that the County should terminate his contract as a penalty for being histrionic on the field against England and for berating a journalist when he should have been on the field. Glamorgan, quite rightly, deemed these events none of their business.

Viv's arrival added thousands to the county income from members, sponsors and box-holders even before he picked up a bat for the County.

He was made to feel at home immediately in the dressing room and outside. Within 24 hours, he had picked up a bat and though it was not the most auspicious of starts, by the end of the day, all was forgiven, as he took the wicket of Dermot Reeve, l.b.w. to one of his 'trundlers' with the last ball of the Benson and Hedges Cup game at Edgbaston with just three runs needed!

Perhaps his most remarkable contribution in the summer of 1990 came in the Championship match with Hampshire at Southampton. Glamorgan were chasing a target of 363 and at tea, they were a modest 139 for five and a draw or a Hampshire victory seemed very likely. There then followed a quite outstanding batting performance from the West Indian. Initially, he had been quite content to push ones and twos and he reached the final hour of the game with 112 needed for victory. Picking up the tempo, first with Nigel Cowley and then Colin Metson, the target became 27 needed from the last two overs. After a fruitful penultimate over, Richards was left to face the last over with 12 runs needed for victory – the bowler, Malcolm Marshall. He settled the issue in superb style, with a drive for four, an enormous hook for six and another four, despite the fact that Hampshire had nine men back on the boundary!

Against Warwickshire at St Helen's, off-spinner Adrian Pierson was getting quite a bit of assistance from the pitch, and forced Richards to play an on-drive too early, the ball ending up at mid-off. The audacious young spinner immediately told the Glamorgan batsman where the shot should have gone – the next ball he bowled was deposited onto the roof of the Swansea pavilion.

One of Viv Richards's personal assets is pride and he showed it during Glamorgan's two encounters with Essex. At Ilford in mid-June in a Sunday League game, he was out first ball and was met with a torrent of abuse from a section of the Essex crowd. When the Welsh County returned to Essex for the Championship game at Southend two months later, he was eager to show the Essex fans that he had not lost his touch and scored 111 and 118 not out.

Although illness kept him out of the last few matches of the 1990 season and prevented him attacking the £10,000 National Power 50-sixes jackpot, Viv Richards rounded off a successful season with Glamorgan, for whom he scored over 2,000 runs in all matches, by hitting the most sixes in the country.

He had began the season by saying that 1990 would be his last in county cricket, but after club officials had offered him new terms for a further three years, he accepted, saying he would play in 1992 and 1993.

In the summer of 1991, he led the West Indies in the five-match Test series, one of the most enthralling in living memory.

Viv made a brief visit to Cardiff during the winter of 1991-92 to confirm that he would be returning for the following season, despite not being included in the West Indies Cup squad.

Glamorgan remained delighted by the reliability of Viv Richards and in his last season saw the West Indies score an unbeaten 224 against Middlesex at Cardiff.

It was great to see him bow out at Canterbury, not with one of his greatest innings, but with majesty, dignity and a little of the infamous strut and swagger, as he guided Glamorgan to their first title for 24 years. His enthusiasm remained undimmed and his loyalty to his team as strong and committed as ever.

An amusing contrast came in the form of a tale concernng Abdul Quadir, who in 1989 received a letter from Glamorgan enquiring if he would be interested in becoming their overseas player. The reply duly arrived – in January 1992!

NORMAN RICHES

Born: 9th June, 1883. Cardiff
Died: 6th November, 1975
Played: 1901-1934

FIRST-CLASS GLAMORGAN RECORD

Innings	Not Out	Runs	H.Sc.	Average	100's
362	38	11722	217*	36.18	20

Overs	Mdns	Runs	Wkts	Average	Best
27.3	1	101	1	101.00	1-4

NOTABLE FEATS
- He scored 217* v. Dorset at Blandford in 1907.
- He scored 1,000 runs in a season for Glamorgan in their first year in the County Championship.
- After the County achieved first-class status, he carried his bat for Glamorgan on two occasions, with a best of 177* out of 347 v. Leicestershire at Leicester in 1921.
- In 1928, he scored 538 runs at 59.77.

NORMAN VAUGHAN RICHES is on record as saying that his first recollection of the game was of W. G. Grace playing at Cardiff Arms Park when he was eight years old.

A dentist by profession, Riches was associated with Glamorgan all his life as a cricketer, captain, administrator and finally, Presi-

dent. He first played for Glamorgan in 1901 and in the next 19 years scored heavily in the Minor County Championship. Destined to play one of the greatest parts in Glamorgan's history and to be the main factor leading to the County attaining first-class status, he was in good form in 1904, scoring 491 runs with a top score of 183 and an average of 43.10. Riches was the first to carry his bat through a completed innings, scoring 178 not out in a total of 357 against Northumberland at Cardiff on June 26th-27th 1906. The following summer saw him top the averages again, with 613 runs at 51.08 and a top score of 217 not out. He was in fine form in 1910, but contracted enteric fever and was unwell for several weeks. Despite Glamorgan's poor results in 1911, it was an outstanding year for Norman Riches. He set up a new Minor County record by scoring 1,005 runs at an average of 92.27. He hit two centuries against Monmouthshire, plus 150 in the game against Carmarthenshire, but his highest and best innings came against Buckinghamshire at Neath. His innings was described by the *Western Mail:* 'When the loose ball comes along, he revels in putting the full face of the bat hard against it. Perfect footwork, perfect timing, an elegant flash of the bat and the score-box is ringing up another four.'

He captained Wales against M.C.C., of which club he was also a playing member.

In 1920, Glamorgan played the M.C.C. in a friendly at St Helen's, with Riches leading by example, sharing a century partnership with Whittington for the first wicket. Riches also played for the Minor Counties that season in their annual game against the M.C.C. and hit a magnificent 147. Norman Riches captained the Glamorgan side in their first year as a first-class county, and was the only batsman to score 1,000 runs. He led the side to a 23-run victory in their opening match with Sussex and had he been able to devote more of his time to the game he must have been a candidate for Test matches.

There are many who would go as far as to say that Norman Riches was the best amateur batsman to be produced in South Wales – certainly up to the end of his playing career. In fact, of him, J. C. Clay said: 'He was the only batsman with the skill and application to get runs regularly at first-class level.'

As a batsman, he possessed a sound technique and temperament and a wide range of shots, especially off his legs. He combined an impenetrable defence on the worst of wickets with intense powers of concentration and yet at the same time, was not a slow scorer. Riches was also the master of the tactical single designed to bring about a readjustment of the field, and having achieved this objective, took particular pleasure to smash a boundary through the gap he had created.

He was a beautiful fielder, whether in the cover or the deep and a very competent wicket-keeper, though being a dentist, he was reluctant to keep, except in an emergency, for fear of damaging his hands!

Because of his increasing involvement in his family's dental practice, he decided to stand down as captain for the 1922 season. In fact, he only played in 11 games, but still scored 561 runs at an average of 33.00 and a top score of 128 against Worcestershire.

In 1924, he made a superb 170 in the match against Derbyshire as Glamorgan won by an innings, but his highest first-class score for the County, 177 not out, was made against Leicestershire in the Club's inaugural season as a first-class county. Though he was only able to play in a few matches in 1925, he was one of three Glamorgan players chosen to represent Wales against the M.C.C. at Lord's. The M.C.C. batted first and scored 532, but Wales could only total 328 and batted again 204 runs behind. At this point, Riches then in his 42nd year, batted right through the second innings to score 187 not out from Wales's total of 411 for five. In 1926, he made one of his rare appearances for the County against Derbyshire in the first game to be played at Pontypridd, scoring 136 in a stay of nearly three-and-a-half hours. That season, he also played for Wales, making an unbeaten 239 against Ireland in Belfast.

Riches was considered for an M.C.C. tour to the West Indies in the late 1920's and a senior Glamorgan official was contacted to see if Riches was available. His reply was: 'It's no good asking him as he wouldn't have the time to go.' But ironically, he would have jumped at the opportunity and got time off had he been approached.

There were suggestions that his limited appearances for Glamorgan meant that he was picking his matches in order to avoid the stronger bowling sides and in particular the sides which possessed really fast bowlers. These insinuations were refuted in 1928 when, at the age of 45, he played a superb innings of 140 against Lancashire at Old Trafford – this against an attack that contained Ted McDonald, Dick Tyldesley and Cecil Parkin.

In 1934, the injury crisis at the club was so severe that Riches was recalled for the match against Worcestershire at 51 years of age. It was the final appearance of a batsman of real class in what was often a weak Glamorgan side. In the circumstances, his record over these 13 years of 4,419 runs with an average of 33.99 is remarkable, and gives some idea of what he might have accomplished some 20 years earlier. He maintained close links with the County by serving on the committee and acting as a Trustee, though in 1925, he made just one appearance in the Minor County Championship and scored 114!

He died on 6th November 1975 at the age of 92, the last surviving Glamorgan link with Minor County days.

FRANK RYAN

Born: 14th November, 1888.
New Jersey
Died: 5th January, 1954
Played: 1922-1931

FIRST-CLASS GLAMORGAN RECORD

Innings	Not Out	Runs
312	100	1699
H.Sc.	Average	100's
46	8.01	–

Overs	Mdns	Runs	Wkts	Average	Best
6,589.2	1317	19053	913	20.86	8-41

NOTABLE FEATS
- He took 100 wickets in a season for Glamorgan on five occasions, with a best of 133 at 17.46 each in 1925.
- He took eight for 41 v. Derbyshire in 1925.

Frank Ryan was an erratic genius, who, on his day and given the right wicket, would bowl out any side in the country.

His background was both mysterious and unusual. Born in New Jersey, U.S.A. on November 14th 1888, he came to England at an early age and was educated at Bedford Grammar School. Following service in the Royal Flying Corps during the First World War, he began his first-class career with Hampshire in 1919. But, after two seasons in which he played in 23 matches, taking 63 wickets at 26.09, he turned to Lancashire League cricket, before joining Glamorgan in 1922.

Something of an eccentric, he hitch-hiked his way from Hampshire and was completely penniless when he arrived in South Wales to seek out a new cricketing career.

Making his Glamorgan debut in 1922, he took eight wickets in his solitary appearance for the County. In 1923, he was able to play on a regular basis and showed his worth by taking 106 wickets at an average of 22.53, including five wickets in an innings on eight occasions, to become the first Glamorgan player to complete 100 wickets in a season. There are many stories about Ryan's activities and habits – one of the best concerning his late arrival for the match with Somerset at Cardiff that season. Glamorgan had played Lancashire in the previous match and been beaten by an innings and 220 runs. Frank Ryan stayed on at Blackpool with some Lancastrian friends after the match, while the rest of the team returned by train to Cardiff. In the early hours of the morning, Ryan hired a taxi and arrived at the Arms Park at 11.10 the next morning, entering the dressing room with the wonderful phrase 'Ryan never lets you down'!

Like so many other slow left-arm bowlers, at times he reached the heights of being unplayable, his natural leg-break resulting frequently in success to his side. Tall, with a high easy action, he not only spun the ball considerably, but maintained great accuracy. With his arrival, the County's attack increased in effectiveness and in 1924, he dismissed 120 batsmen for 14.58 runs each. This was his most successful season to date, with his feats including six for 17 and six for 48 v. Somerset at Taunton; six for 46 and five for 18 v. Leicestershire and four for 69 and six for 40 v. Lancashire, both at Swansea. In this latter match, he was tossed the ball and J. C. Clay who always had great faith in Ryan said: 'Now Frank, it's now or never.' Lancashire were 83 for 3 and chasing 146 to win. Bringing the ball down from a great height, Ryan spun it like a top on the dusty surface and the last seven Lancashire wickets crashed for 23 runs, Ryan taking five of them for 11.

In 1925, he took 133 wickets at 17.46, with 37 of them coming in a three-match spell, which included 14 for 165 against Essex at Swansea and his career-best figures of eight for 41 against Derbyshire – they would have been ever better but for the fact that both G. M. Lee and S. Cadman, Derbyshire's two top scorers, were missed off his bowling.

In the middle, Ryan never took his batting seriously – his highest score in 312 innings being 46. There is one story of Frank Ryan that if true, shows his attitude towards batting. Harold Larwood of Nottinghamshire and England was bowling at his fastest. The first two balls whizzed past Frank's bat, as he swept the air.

Then, as the third was being bowled, he hit his own wicket with a resounding smack at the same time going through the motions of one of cricket's most unorthodox strokes. As he returned to the pavilion, the Trent Bridge members sympathized with him, 'Bad luck old boy.' 'Bad luck indeed,' said Frank once in the dressing room. 'It was jolly good luck. Fancy standing up to Larwood for half an hour.'

In 1927, by taking nine wickets for 95 runs, he played a large part in the defeat by an innings and 81 runs at Swansea of Nottinghamshire – it was the last game of the season; the sensational result enabling Lancashire to snatch the County Championship title.

The following summer, he ended the season with 86 wickets at 28.15, but this total flattered him somewhat, for he bowled poorly in the early part of the season. In fact, at one stage, the Glamorgan committee decided not to offer him a new contract, but they were forced to change their mind later in the season, as he turned in some very useful performances. Ryan had a liking for the demon drink – apparently after one lengthy drinking session after a day's play, he forgot where the team was staying and returned to the ground to sleep under the covers!

It was Frank Ryan who, to the most deafening roar to emit from a Welsh stadium for many a year, bowled Don Bradman, as the near-miraculous prelude to routing the rest of the Australian side on a never-to-be-forgotten August Bank Holiday at Swansea in 1930. He ended the innings with figures of six for 76 from 34 overs, but at the time he bowled Bradman, his analysis read:

O.	M.	R.	W.
14	3	21	6

At the end of the 1931 season, the Club decided to release Ryan. It must have been a very difficult decision, for Frank Ryan had bowled his heart out for the Welsh side for nine seasons. His departure was not a unanimously popular one, though by now, he was nearing 44 and wasn't the force he had been in previous years.

His aggregate of 913 wickets for the Welsh side were at a cost of 20.86 runs each.

He later took part in South Wales League, Yorkshire Council and Lancashire League cricket. Ryan, who had a keen eye for women, fell prey to drugs, but survived to become an inspector for the War Graves Commission after the Second World War.

He died at Leicester on January 5th 1954, aged 65, one of the best slow left-arm bowlers of his day.

RAVI SHASTRI

Born: 27th May, 1962. Bombay
Played: 1987-1991

FIRST-CLASS GLAMORGAN RECORD

Innings	Not Out	Runs	H.Sc.	Average	100's
99	18	3442	157	42.49	6

Overs	Mdns	Runs	Wkts	Average	Best
1,313.4	341	3264	96	34.00	7-49

NOTABLE FEATS
- He hit 157 v. Somerset at Cardiff in 1988.
- He took seven for 49 v. Lancashire at Swansea in 1988.
- He scored 200* in 113 minutes, including 6 sixes off one over whilst playing for Bombay v. Baroda.
- He scored 127 and 101* v. Middlesex at Abergavenny in 1989.

RAVINSHAKAR JAYDRITHA SHASTRI made his debut for Bombay in 1979 and played his first Test match when only 18-years-old. He took 15 wickets in his first three Tests and has not often been omitted from the India side since then. At the time of writing, he has played in 73 Tests, scoring 3,460 runs and capturing 143 wickets.

His Test career certainly had an eventful start. In February 1981, while the Indian team was on a tour of Australia and New Zealand, Shastri was at home, helping Bombay qualify for the final stages of the Ranji Trophy. Against Baroda he scored 58 and took four for 41 and four for 17 against Gujarat. During the next match against Uttar Pradesh, he received a telegram from India's captain Gavaskar telling him he was needed in New Zealand. In fact, Shastri had contrived to get two 'ducks' in Bombay's totals of 441 and 327 for six and had not taken a wicket!

Catching the first plane out, he arrived in the windy city of Wellington on the eve of the first Test, to be told he was in the side. He finished with three for 54 in the first innings, including the last two wickets in two balls. His first Test innings saw him bat at No.10, his first scoring shot resulting in the run out of his partner as they attempted a fourth run!

New Zealand were 152 ahead on the first innings and 99 for seven in their second innings when Shastri began a new over. At the end of it, they were 100 all out – Shastri having taken three wickets in four deliveries. Two matches later, having retained his place, despite Doshi's return, he bowled 56 overs in the New Zealand first innings at Auckland and took five for 125.

Except John Wright, Shastri dismissed every batsman in the New Zealand line-up at least once. He ended the three-match series with 15 wickets and had the statisticians looking for parallels when a player had gone straight into a Test match after a 36-hour flight. Gary Sobers had done it before – but he wasn't 18 and wasn't playing in his first Test!

As a bowler, Shastri was of a different breed to many of his predecessors. Of course, he was conditioned by the heavy demand on economy in one-day cricket and so he tended to bowl flat and relatively fast, concentrating on the batsman's pads and unless the ball was turning, he operated to a leg-side field.

During England's visit to India in 1984-85, his batting took over to such an extent that he scored two centuries in the series and averaged over 50. He started with 142 in the Bombay Test which India won, but it was at Calcutta, where he angered even his own countrymen. He took six hours getting to 90 and then spent another hour crawling along to his fourth Test hundred.

Happy to return to Bombay, he played at the Wankhede Stadium against Baroda in a Ranji Trophy match. Gavaskar was probably considering a declaration when Shastri strode to the wicket, a heavier bat swinging from his hand. Within 71 minutes, he had reached his hundred, though he had been dropped four times, but it was his second century which saw him timing the ball to perfection to hit cleanly, and taking only a further 42 minutes to reach 200. When he was on 147, he faced left-arm spinner Tilak Raj. Hitting the first ball straight for six, he despatched the next two over long-on before hitting the fourth, which was pitched down the leg-side over square leg. The fifth ball became the third to clear long-on and he now faced up to the last ball with Gary Sobers's record in sight. Raj bowled wider of the off stump, but Shastri was quickly in position and the sixth flew at the sightscreen. His double century arrived in 113 minutes – the fastest of all time, beating Gilbert Jessop and Clive Lloyd's double-hundred record and equalling Sober's six sixes – not bad for a player who entered Test cricket as a left-arm spinner batting at No.10.

Joining Glamorgan in 1987, he quickly settled in, hitting his highest score in the County Championship, 157, in the match against Somerset at Cardiff the following season. A season in which I witnessed his best ever bowling figures for the County, seven for 49 against Lancashire at Swansea.

Against Middlesex at Abergavenny in June 1989, he hit 127 in the first innings, as he and Alan Butcher added 216 for the fourth wicket and then an unbeaten 101 in the second – his 100 coming off 117 balls with four sixes and 16 fours. His one-day talents were seen in the Sunday League fixture against the same county, when he hit 92 and took three for 33. An all-round influence in the Glamorgan side's improvement in 1989, Shastri was busy with the Indian tourists in 1990, touring England. He scored 336 runs in the three match series, including 187 in the final Test at the Oval.

In 1991, again with Middlesex the opponents, he did not bowl an over through a crisis of confidence, though before the season began, he was open to Glamorgan about his worries. He did however volunteer to bowl in the first-class game against Cambridge University and with some success. He continued to practise in the nets and finished the season with 27 wickets at 26.07 to head the County bowling averages!

During the 1991 season, there was further evidence of his big hitting when, in the match against Warwickshire at Edgbaston, he hit a quickfire 80 not out – an innings that contained three sixes and 10 fours.

Glamorgan though probably expected a few more runs from Ravi Shastri. His international pedigree wasn't paraded as impressively as it might have been.

DON SHEPHERD

Born: 12th August, 1927. Port Eynon
Played: 1950-1972

FIRST-CLASS GLAMORGAN RECORD

Innings	Not Out	Runs	H.Sc.	Average	100's
816	241	5610	73	9.75	–

Overs	Mdns	Runs	Wkts	Average	Best
21514.2	7334	45571	2174	20.95	9-47

NOTABLE FEATS

- He took nine for 47 v. Northamptonshire at the Arms Park in 1954 and nine for 48 v. Yorkshire at Swansea in 1965.
- He took over 100 wickets in a season for Glamorgan on 12 occasions with a best of 168 at 14.03 runs each in 1956.
- He holds the Glamorgan record for the earliest date in taking 100 wickets in a season – 2nd July 1956.
- He has bowled the most balls in an innings for Glamorgan – 346 in the match against Derbyshire at Swansea to finish with the following figures:

O.	M.	R.	W.
57.4	26	106	6

- He scored 26 runs off one over from E. Smith of Derbyshire at the Arms Park in 1961.
- He hit 57* in 15 minutes v. Australia at Swansea in 1961, in just eleven scoring strokes.
- He performed the hat-trick v. Northamptonshire at Swansea in 1964.
- He took seven for 7 v. Hampshire at the Arms Park in 1966.
- In 1968, he bowled 12 maiden overs in succession v. Hampshire at Southampton.

MOST CRICKET FOLLOWERS, when asked to name their best side of players who never represented England, would have the name of Don Shepherd high on their list.

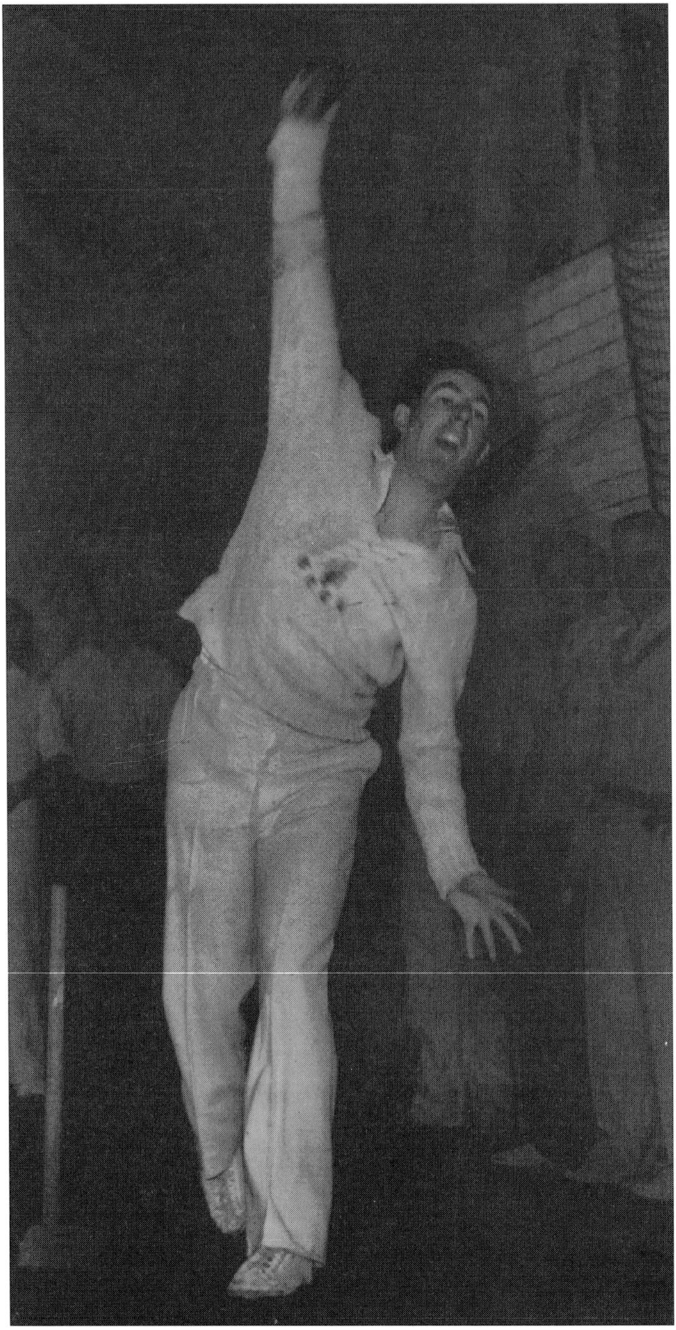

DON SHEPHERD

Born at Port Eynon, a remote village in the Gower peninsula some eighteen miles from Swansea, he had little early ambitions as a cricketer and his father, always busy in the family business, had little time to encourage him. His grandfather was probably his earliest association with the game, for the old gentleman frequently scored for the village side while Don sat with him. There were few games for him at the Gowerton Boys' School and it was not until his days in the forces that he rapidly developed his natural ability.

During service at R.A.F. Detford with the Fleet Air Arm, he played for the station side against Worcestershire II and the Gentlemen of Worcestershire at Pershore. His bowling impressed Major Jewell, the former Worcestershire captain, and Shepherd was given a trial and offered a contract. Word soon reached the ears of the Glamorgan officials that a young Welsh bowler might be joining Worcestershire. Glamorgan coach George Lavis had a word with 'Shep' who accepted the Welsh County's offer.

In 1948, he became a professional player on the M.C.C. ground staff at Lord's, playing his first game for the Glamorgan Second Eleven against Devonshire at Exeter in the late summer. It was an inauspicious start for though he bowled a long spell of thirty overs, he ended with 0 for 61. The following year he returned home to play in the County second team and for Swansea in the South Wales and Monmouthshire League, an apprenticeship which was to give him the background for his long service with Glamorgan.

He made his first-class debut for the County at the Oval in 1950 and following that initial game, he was rarely out of the side. In 1952, he took 115 wickets with his fast-medium deliveries of commendable line and length. He returned to Lord's to open the bowling for Glamorgan against Middlesex and in his opening spell dismissed Brown, Edrich and Compton cheaply, but then dropped Jack Robertson off his own bowling! He earned his County cap, but was not really satisfied that he was producing his maximum effect for he lacked the real fire of a pace bowler.

Yet in 1954, he took a career best nine for 47 as Northants were beaten by 262 runs at the Arms Park.

By August 1955 he had taken only 40 wickets and so, after seeking advice from Wilf Wooller and Haydn Davies, he spent many hours in the nets experimenting with off-cutters that was shortly to produce in him the ultimate in effectiveness. The change proved a huge success for in the final game of the season against Worcestershire at Neath, he took ten for 85.

He still retained the high elegant action, though he bowled a finger spin of near medium pace. His style suited the typical English wickets on which he had to bowl, for on the slow turning track his extra pace gave the batsmen less time to play their strokes and his precise line and length with the occasional change of flight and pace made him a reliable defensive bowler who could tie up one end on a plumb wicket.

'Shep' always insisted on the wicket-keeper standing back, yet there was a time at the Scarborough Festival when Godfrey Evans, standing up, missed an outside edge and denied him a hat-trick!

His first full season as a quick spinner was startling and only rain, which washed out Nottinghamshire's second innings at Trent Bridge at the end of June, prevented him taking 100 wickets before July. He was though the first bowler in the country to take over a hundred wickets and finished up with 168 at an average of only 14.03, the best for the Club since 1937. His best performance came at the Arms Park in June, when he took twelve for 64 in an eight-wicket win over Hampshire. He played a leading role in the return fixture at Bournemouth, as the home side were dismissed for 90, when chasing 293, with 'Shep' returning the remarkable figures of:

O.	M.	R.	W.
16	11	6	4

In 1960, he took 142 wickets at 17.52 apiece. He played a great part in the County's excellent win over Yorkshire, as Glamorgan won by 72 runs, by taking five for 52 in the first innings. He took eleven wickets against Warwickshire and had eight for 45 against the South Africans, both on his 'home' ground at St Helens.

He was an aggressive lower-order batsman who frequently launched a series of famous assaults on the bowling. Some of his exhibitions were close to the sensational, such as his 73 against Derbyshire, when in one over, he hit Edwin Smith for 26 and hit 52 in sixteen minutes. At Swansea, he was top scorer when going in last against Gloucestershire and one of his towering sixes climbed clear over the rugby stand! In 1961, he scored a half-century with just eleven scoring strokes in 15 minutes against the Australians.

In the match against Australia in 1964, he was one of the architects of the Welsh side's 36 run win. His bowling figures are worth recording:

O.	M.	R.	W.		O.	M.	R.	W.
17	12	22	4	and	52	29	71	5

Also that season, the damp conditions in the match against Leicestershire at Ebbw Vale helped 'Shep' to turn in the remarkable analysis of:

O.	M.	R.	W.
10	8	2	5

The Grace Road outfit had been set 149 in 110 minutes, but were dismissed for just 33 runs in the space of 80 minutes.

Replacing the indisposed Tony Lewis for the match against the Australians in 1968, the game was a triumph for Don Shepherd as his subtle tactics and clever bowling changes brought victory to Glamorgan by 79 runs. It was 'Shep's' only regret that the County never asked him to captain the side when Tony Lewis prematurely retired in the early 1970s. Yet he enjoyed every minute of his long career and never gave less than 100% to his team. He was a great as set to successive Glamorgan captains in his role as senior professional.

Possessing the great ability of being able to undercut the ball and make it move in the air to deceive a batsman, making him think it was an off-break, only to edge it into the slips or to the wicket-keeper, he took 106 wickets in 1970 to top the national bowling averages.

His last match for Glamorgan came in 1972 against Worcestershire in a Sunday League fixture at Colwyn Bay. As he hung up his boots to retire, he had captured 2,174 wickets – more than any other cricketer not to play in Tests – few of his victims would not have been prepared to grant that he would not have disgraced England in international cricket.

Since his retirement, he has been a Justice of the Peace and in 1979 was awarded the Queen's Silver Jubilee medal for sport. 'Shep's' experience has not been lost to the Club for he now combines his duties as a radio commentator with a role as Glamorgan's bowling adviser.

During his playing career, cricket's highest honours never came to Don Shepherd, though he was made an honorary life member of the M.C.C. in 1992, but as Richie Benaud once said of him: 'Had he been an Australian, he would have played for his country many many times.'

CYRIL SMART

Born: 23rd July, 1898. Lacock, Wiltshire
Died: 21st May, 1975
Played: 1927-1946

FIRST-CLASS GLAMORGAN RECORD

Innings	Not Out	Runs
301	35	8069
H.Sc.	Average	100's
151*	30.34	9

Overs	Mdns	Runs	Wkts	Average	Best
2097.4	302	6943	169	41.08	5-39

NOTABLE FEATS
- He scored 1,000 runs in a season for Glamorgan on 5 occasions.
- He scored 32 runs off one over bowled by G. Hill of Hampshire at the Arms Park in 1935.

UNABLE TO COMMAND a regular place in the Warwickshire XI of the early 1920s (he played in 45 matches with a highest score of 59 and his nine wickets cost him 56.44 runs each) he migrated to South Wales as a professional with the Briton Ferry Steelworks Club. Playing in the 'old pros' burial ground of the South Wales and Monmouthshire League, he soon began to establish himself as one of the League's greatest entertainers as an opening batsman in the Charlie Barnett/Harold Gimblett mould. It was Maurice Turnbull who resurrected the neglected genius of Smart, for he was keen to get back into first-class cricket on a regular basis. However, he wasn't much of a success during a number of appearances for Glamorgan between 1927 and 1933, where his top score was only 45. In fact, it wasn't until 1934, when he was 36, that Smart was summoned to reinforce the inexperienced ranks of the fast-emerging Glamorgan side on a regular basis.

He enjoyed great success in his first full season in the County team, scoring 1,335 runs at an average of 37.08, during which he hit his maiden first-class century, 128 in the match against Worcestershire at Cardiff. His free hitting was a joy to watch and gave the tail the confidence it had lacked previously.

In the words of J. C. Clay, 'the flower of Cyril Smart's batsmanship burst into bloom when many of his contemporaries were fading. He was an autumn crocus.' It was a wonderful way of describing the rugged exterior of a genuine professional who was on his day as competent a hard-hitting number six batsman as one could wish to see. His performances suggested that Warwickshire and Glamorgan (where his talents had languished in Welsh club cricket) had both overlooked a potential star.

Cyril Smart was a crowd pleaser, immediately seizing the chance to demonstrate that as a scientific hitter of a cricket ball, he deserved to rank alongside Gilbert Jessop and Keith Miller. He loved to hit the ball hard, back over the bowler's head; but he could also defend with a very straight bat. He wasn't a big man, but he possessed a natural gift of timing, enabling him to hit the ball with a smooth action which seemed effortless.

In 1935, he topped the Glamorgan batting averages with 1,559 runs at 36.25. The Hampshire visit to Cardiff was celebrated by the performance of Cyril Smart. During his innings of 109, he hit Hampshire's Gerry Hill for 32 runs off one over – it was at the time a world record – the greatest number of runs ever scored off a six-ball over. This is how the over went – 6, 6, 4, 6, 6, 4 – Alletson's feat of 34 runs off an over in 1911 for Nottinghamshire was performed off seven balls, one a no-ball. Smart's innings was one of the greatest exhibitions of hitting ever, and put the Glamorgan players in top gear, for a ten wicket victory followed.

The County gained a surprising victory at Hastings against a strong Sussex team, winning by three wickets, after a fight for runs in little time in the fourth innings. Glamorgan were left to score 165 runs to win in 105 minutes, the runs being made with three wickets in hand off what was the last over of the game. In Glamorgan's first innings, Cyril Smart had scored well, his unbeaten 151 being made in three hours and included six sixes – it was his highest score for Glamorgan.

The Whitsun match at Cardiff against the South African touring team provided one of the sensational matches for which the County is remembered. The tourists batted first and lost Bruce Mitchell quickly, but Wade and Rowan stayed together for over four hours, adding 256 for the second wicket, the score at the close of play being 327 for three. On the Monday morning, Glamorgan got the last seven wickets down early, for the conditions favoured the bowlers more – the tourists innings ending on 401. Glamorgan then collapsed in less than three hours and were all out for 142. Following-on, 259 runs behind, four wickets were lost for 10 runs by the close of play, the position of the County appearing hopeless. On the last day, the fifth wicket fell at 10, and though wickets fell steadily, Smart offered plenty of resistance until the ninth wicket fell at 114. All seemed lost when Smart was joined by Donald Hughes, a 25-year-old schoolmaster making his County debut. To the great surprise and delight of the spectators, they proceeded to thrash the tourists' bowling all round the field, adding an unbeaten 131 for the last wicket in an hour to force a draw, for a rain storm broke over the ground to prevent further play. Smart scored 114 not out and soon after reaching his century, he lofted one ball clean out of the ground and through the window of the nearby Grand Hotel in Westgate Street!

His exceptional batting that season resulted in his hitting 30 sixes – an unusually high aggregate for a batsman as against a huge hitter.

As the occasion demanded, he offered the batsman a gentle species of leg-spin which brought him 169 wickets at 41.08.

One of Glamorgan's mightiest hitters, Cyril Smart was a quiet unassuming man, who was never far from a cricket field for the rest of his life.

GREG THOMAS

Born: 12th August, 1960
Played: 1979-1988

FIRST-CLASS GLAMORGAN RECORD

Innings	Not Out	Runs	H.Sc.	Average	100's
139	24	2137	110	18.58	2

Overs	Mdns	Runs	Wkts	Average	Best
2244.5	386	8230	256	32.15	6.68

NOTABLE FEATS
- He took five for 17 v. Sussex at Sophia Gardens in the 1985 Nat West Competition.
- He scored two first-class hundreds in 1988, with a best of 110 in the match v. Warwickshire at Edgbaston.

HAILING FROM TREBANOS in the Tawe Valley, Greg Thomas began playing junior cricket with the village team before progressing to Clydach and Landore in the South Wales leagues. Greg quickly built up a good reputation and turned in several very impressive performances with both bat and ball in the local leagues, and on his appearances for Swansea Schoolboys and the Welsh Schools' team.

When he was 14-years-old, he appeared for Glamorgan Colts and the following year played for a Glamorgan XI in a friendly match. During the school holidays, he regularly played for the Colts team and made several appearances for the County Second Eleven.

Like many other youngsters in the Welsh valleys, he was a talented school rugby player. He represented Glamorgan Under-19s as a number eight or flank forward and took part in the final trials of the Welsh Under-19 team.

After leaving Cwmtawe Comprehensive School in Pontardawe, he attended South Glamorgan Institute of Higher Education to obtain a teaching qualification. While still at Cardiff College, he made his first-class debut for Glamorgan in 1979 in the match against the touring Sri Lankans at Swansea.

In 1980, he sustained a back injury and had to undergo surgery at the end of the season for a stress fracture. However, he confirmed his promise the following season by helping the County win the Under-25 title. Surprisingly, it was not a bowling performance which first brought Greg Thomas recognition in the national press. During Glamorgan's first innings in their game against Surrey at Guildford in 1982, he went in at number seven and made a quickfire 84 before being bowled by Sylvester Clarke. That innings remained his highest first-class score until 1988 when he hit two centuries.

As a bowler, Thomas had a very smooth and flowing side-on action, delivering the ball from close to the stumps. He was capable of bursts of high quality, bowling at blistering pace. Unfortunately, he was also likely to lose all control of his line, length and rhythm, but in 1984, he achieved his first ten-wicket haul in a thrilling two-wicket win over Somerset at Cardiff. It was a season in which he began to bowl with sustained pace and hostility, proving that he had fully recovered from the sprinkling of injuries which had affected him earlier in his career. When Thomas was out playing for Border in South Africa under the guidance of Rodney Ontong, the Glamorgan committee decided to dispense with the services of West Indian star Winston Davis.

Having the opportunity to open the Glamorgan bowling on a regular basis, he began to produce performances that completely justified the Welsh County's committee's faith in him as a genuine fast bowler. One of his fastest spells in that summer of 1985 came in the match against Hampshire at Southampton in front of Alan Smith, the ex-Warwickshire wicket-keeper and then England Test selector. Thomas hurried all the Hampshire top-order with his pace and lift off a relatively easy paced wicket. However, from mid-June onwards, he faced one niggling injury after another and ended the season with a modest haul of 34 wickets at 32.47 each. Nevertheless, he had shown enough promise and had clearly impressed Alan Smith, and he was chosen for England's winter tour to the West Indies.

Greg's only worry was his tendency to incur minor injuries, so in the months leading up to Christmas, he worked hard at building up his fitness by running in the hills around his home in the Swansea Valley, training with his local rugby team and bowling in the nets at the Neath Indoor Cricket School.

Labelled 'the fastest white man in county cricket' he made his Test debut at Kingston. There was almost a first ball wicket for him as Desmond Haynes edged the ball head high between first and second slip and was then dropped by Peter Willey in the gully off the second! Thomas gained his revenge by having Haynes caught behind in his second spell and though he ended the series with 8 wickets at 45.50 and was dropped for the last match of the series after a disappointing performance in the fourth Test at Port-of-Spain, he returned home full of optimism and with a growing reputation.

He did build on his success in the Caribbean, but was still affected by niggling injuries and frustrated by the lifeless Welsh wickets – both of which hampered his claims for a regular Test spot – and he finished with 39 wickets in the Championship.

Against Somerset at Taunton he was at the peak of his form and sent some balls flying past Viv Richards's nose. After one particularly quickish delivery, Thomas glared down the track at Viv and said: 'It's red, it's round and it's fast.' A few overs later, Richards stepped away to leg and smashed Thomas over the stands and into the nearby river saying, 'Hey man, you know what it looks like, you go and find it!'

By the end of the 1987 season, Greg Thomas had become disillusioned at having to bowl on slow Welsh wickets and asked to be released from his contract, which still had a year to run. The Glamorgan committee did not want to lose the talented fast bowler and so refused to let him join another county for 1988.

Against Surrey that summer, he produced a match-winning spell at Ebbw Vale as the visitors chased a target of 198. Bowling very fast and to a full length, he took the last three wickets in the space of six balls to leave Surrey eight runs short of victory.

It was his last season with the Welsh county and though the soft pitches of South Wales were never suited to the pace bowler (he never achieved 50 Championship wickets in a season) his batting in the lower-order developed to such an extent that in 1988, he scored two centuries, with a best of 110 against Warwickshire at Edgbaston.

Moving to Northamptonshire, the England selectors were hoping that he would be inspired to realise his true potential as a strike bowler. In 1989, he took 66 wickets at 28.27, but then joined Mike Gatting's ill-fated 'rebel' tour of South Africa in 1989-90 to end his Test playing days.

After playing in just ten matches in 1991, he was forced to retire from the game. He had always struggled with injury problems and doctors diagnosed arthritis in his left hip. In all first-class matches, the 'Trebanos Terror' took 525 wickets at 31.20 with a best bowling performance of seven for 75 against his old county in 1990!

MAURICE TURNBULL

Born: 16th March, 1906. Cardiff
Died: 5th August, 1944
Played: 1924-1939

FIRST-CLASS GLAMORGAN RECORD

Innings	Not Out	Runs
504	25	14431
H.Sc.	Average	100's
233	30.12	22

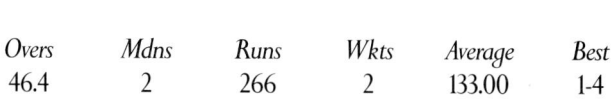

Overs	Mdns	Runs	Wkts	Average	Best
46.4	2	266	2	133.00	1-4

NOTABLE FEATS

- He scored 205 v. Nottinghamshire at Cardiff Arms Park in 1932.
- He scored 200* v. Northamptonshire at Swansea in 1933.
- He scored 1,000 runs in a season for Glamorgan on 8 occasions.
- He holds the record for the fastest double hundred for Glamorgan when he hit 200* v. Worcestershire at Swansea in 1937 in 188 minutes, going on to make a career best of 233.

MAURICE TURNBULL'S FATHER was a wealthy shipowner in Penarth, and together with his seven brothers, he attended Downside School in Somerset. He had a fine record there, averaging 84.7 in 1924 with three centuries, including a school record of 184 inside three hours against King's Bruton. As a result of his outstanding schoolboy record, Johnny Clay invited young Maurice to play for the County during the school holidays.

His first-class debut was against Lancashire at Swansea and the occasion, if anything, was prophetic in that he was immediately called on to perform one of those 'rescue acts' which were to become his speciality in the years ahead. After his more experienced colleagues in the batting order had been swept away by the speed of Ted McDonald, aided by the spin of Cecil Parkin and Dick Tyldesley, he stood fast for 40 hard-won runs, and yet in the nets at Cardiff the day before, he had batted so badly that he wondered if he should stand down. He revealed in that innings the same calculating courage which eight years later enabled him to take a double century off the thunderbolts hurled at him by the Nottinghamshire pair, Larwood and Voce. In 1925, he was still at Downside and scored 1,323 runs at an average of 94.50. The following year, he went up to Cambridge, got his 'Blue' and scored his first century for Glamorgan, 106 not out against Worcestershire at Cardiff. In his last season at Cambridge University, Turnbull scored 1,001 runs at an average of 50, including three centuries, but was unable to force a win in the Varsity match. He joined Glamorgan for the second half of the season and played some useful innings. At the end of the season he was selected for the M.C.C. tour of Australia and New Zealand. He played for England in the Test match at Christchurch – scoring 7 – thus gaining the first Test cap earned by a Glamorgan player. His best innings on the tour was 100 v. New South Wales at Sydney.

Glamorgan sadly lacked a regular captain and by the end of the 1929 season, during which it had seven leaders, the County had a very small membership and were in dire financial trouble. Maurice Turnbull took charge and though success did not come all at once, he improved the playing results and the whole atmosphere within the Club; and this better spirit enabled the County to overcome the financial disaster which was shortly to face it. He linked Monmouthshire with Glamorgan, running a Minor Counties side, and going all out to encourage local talent he not only found players, but widened interest. Encouraging progress was made as the side moved up six places to 11th. Turnbull was in fine form, scoring 1,665 runs, including 160 against Northamptonshire. He was in especially good form in mid-season, passing 50 six times in eight innings. At the end of the season, he left for South Africa with a strong M.C.C. touring team and played in all five Tests, scoring 148 runs in eight innings at an average of 21.14 – his highest score 61 at Johannesburg. His best performance on the tour was 139 against Western Province and he finished the tour with 629 runs to his name. When he combined during the early 1930s the dual role of captain and secretary, things soon began to change for the better. In the beginning he had to rely heavily on the brigade of 'hired mercenaries' like Bates and Bell, Jack Mercer and Frank Ryan – the quartet responding to Turnbull's enthusiasm by producing some of the finest cricket of their, until then, unsung careers.

In his early days, an on-side player, he soon developed all the recognised strokes and a few of his very own, which, though they did not appeal to the purist, were extremely good value for the ordinary spectator – an innings by Maurice Turnbull was a delight to watch!

Perhaps his best innings was his 205 made against Larwood and Voce at Cardiff in the last match of the season. It was rumoured that the Notts opening pair (who had been chosen for the Australian tour) were to try out the fast leg theory bowling which was to cause a rumpus in Australia a few months later. The two held no terrors for Turnbull, as he slashed the rising balls for boundary after boundary. He and Dai Davies added 220 runs in a third-wicket partnership which stood for 16 years. In the same season, on a crumbling Swansea wicket, against Gloucestershire's Goddard and Parker and the clock, he played a magnificent match-winning innings of 119 which enabled Glamorgan to win with ten minutes to spare.

At the end of the 1932 season, Glamorgan were in debt to the tune of about £5,000 and so an appeal was launched – it was largely by Turnbull's personal influence that a sum of £3,500 was raised. He visited almost every town and village in South Wales – night after night Turnbull was working for and shaping the new Glamorgan. He increased the membership and his work in the secretary's office was as valuable to the Club as his greatness on the field of play.

In 1933, he made an unbeaten 200 against Northamptonshire at Swansea. His outstanding performances brought him a return to the England side for the Lord's Test, where he scored 28 as England won by an innings. He was dropped for the next match, but returned for the Oval Test, though he made only 4.

The following summer he topped the Glamorgan averages with 1,302 runs at 42.00 and enjoyed the honour of being appointed captain of the Rest in the Test Trial match at Lord's, but met with little success, scoring only 46 and 29 and seeing his side beaten by ten wickets.

In 1936, he was selected for the Lord's Test after making centuries against Kent and Yorkshire, scoring a duck in the first innings and sharing in an 108 run partnership with Somerset's Harold Gimblett. It was his last Test match, though playing for the South v. North in the Test Trial, scoring a fine century, in a match ruined by rain.

There were few counties playing a more attractive type of cricket than Glamorgan between 1935 and 1939. Turnbull's quick and alert brain was working every minute and had he survived the war, he would most certainly have become captain of England. His wide knowledge was recognised by his appointment as a Test selector.

As a captain, he always got the best out of a moderate side. He could field anywhere, but short-leg was his real position – from what I can gather, the risks he ran and the catches he caught there had to be seen to be believed. Sometimes he literally picked the ball off the defensively held bat, whilst at others, he would cling on to some powerfully hit drives, just a few yards from the bat.

In 1937, he made his highest score of 233 in the match against Worcestershire at Swansea, while two years later, he top scored with 156 in what turned out to be his last innings, against Leicestershire.

On 12th August 1944, a large crowd had gathered to see Glamorgan play the National Fire Service, but they were all stunned into silence at the news of Maurice Turnbull's death. A Major in the Welsh Guards, he was killed in action near Montchamp in Normandy. During an attack, his company got cut off and while making a reconnaissance, he was shot through the head by a sniper and killed instantly.

When he was so cruelly struck down, Maurice Turnbull had scored a total of 14,431 runs for Glamorgan, as well as holding 253 catches with his fearless acrobatics in positions close to the bat.

PETER WALKER

Born: 17th February, 1936. Clifton, Bristol
Played: 1956-1972

FIRST-CLASS GLAMORGAN RECORD

Innings	Not Out	Runs	H.Sc.	Average	100's
738	106	16510	152*	26.12	12

Overs	Mdns	Runs	Wkts	Average	Best
8879.0	2749	21652	771	28.08	7-58

NOTABLE FEATS

- In 1961, in all matches, he achieved the feat of 1,000 runs, 100 wickets and 50 catches. Only one other cricketere, P. G. H. Fender in 1921, has performed the 'treble'.
- He has taken 656 catches for Glamorgan, his best season being 1961 when he took 67 catches.
- He scored 1,000 runs in a season for Glamorgan on 11 occasions.
- In 1969, he bowled 14 maiden overs in succession v. Somerset at Glastonbury.
- He holds the Glamorgan record for the most catches by a fielder in a first-class match, holding 8 against Derbyshire at Swansea in 1970.

PETER WALKER WAS RECOGNISED as a useful spinner, a batsman capable of making a high score and a close catcher who has had no equal in Glamorgan's history. Yet Peter is a man of many facets, broadcaster, journalist, interviewer, author, radio presenter, one time crocodile hunter and in his young days a merchant seaman, a man born in Bristol who has spent much of his life in South Africa, yet who regards himself as owing allegiance to Wales.

When he was only two years of age, his family left Bristol for South Africa where they finally settled in Johannesburg and Peter finished his education at Highlands North High School. Here he failed in his ambition to play junior cricket in the Nuffield Trophy, but did manage to terrify some of the young batsmen with his

quick left-arm bowling off a frighteningly long run. There is no doubt that the young Walker was influenced by Glamorgan players, Dai Davies and Allan Watkins, who coached at Highlands North. It is probably due to his father's association with the Welsh players that Peter Walker came into the county game. It is doubtful whether any other post-war cricketer has entered the game by such a strange route, for his cricket career was initiated just after he left school and was visiting the port of Lorenzo Marques on holiday with a friend. On impulse they signed on as crew members of a Swedish tanker and remained as merchant seamen for more then a year. The tanker travelled between the Persian Gulf and Los Angeles and though the crew were predominantly Finnish, they would wile away the hours on a long journey by holding potato-catching competitions, Young Walker, not wanting to let his country down, would do his utmost not to miss anything catchable! While in dock at Barry, Peter watched Glamorgan playing and resolved to renew his brief acquaintance with Allan Watkins.

The following year, he hitch-hiked to Cardiff to visit his grandfather and whilst there, climbed the stairs of No. 6 High Street, but doubted that they would remember a schoolboy, so he turned and left without knocking. He found his way to the indoor school and after watching the practice for a few moments, spoke to the man who had coached him in South Africa. After twenty minutes batting and bowling, he was offered a two-year contract as a junior professional. However, after his two years were up, his contract was not taken up, though Wilf Wooller still believed he would make a county player and suggested he should return for a summer contract.

He worked his way back from South Africa and in 1957 entered the Glamorgan side as a batsman who also took 33 wickets. The Welsh County had a poor season in 1958, but he scored nearly 1,000 runs and his place in the side was established, not only as a batsman, but as a close catcher. In 1959, he began to mature as an all-rounder, scoring 1,540 runs and capturing 70 wickets. He also took 64 catches to beat Maurice Turnbull's County record and finish as the County's leading fielder. He took some stunning catches – Middlesex looked like snatching victory as Tilly leg-glanced Jim McConnon for what looked like the winning runs, but Walker took off at leg-slip to hold a breathtaking catch with his left hand at full stretch in mid-air. He hit the ground hard but still clung on to the ball and Glamorgan had won by three runs.

In 1960, he was chosen for the first Test against South Africa at Edgbaston. Though he only made 9 in the first innings, he top scored with 37 in the second. Retained for the next match at Lord's, he hit an attractive half-century, followed by 30 in the third Test. However, he had been selected primarily for his spin bowling and as he failed to take any wickets, he was left out to make way for new blood.

After his outstanding success in 1961, when he took 67 catches mostly from the bowling of Don Shepherd, the record for any county, he received a congratulatory telegram from his father worded: 'The Lord is thy Shepherd thou shalt not want'. Walker's overall performance that season was never accorded the publicity it deserved, when he registered probably the best 'treble' ever achieved in cricket, for in addition to his 67 catches, he scored over 1,300 runs and took 101 wickets.

Though he was vulnerable against pace early in his innings, he was an effective, but slightly awkward right-handed batsman – his huge reach enabled him to play forward with ease to smother the danger of most kinds of bowling. Characteristics of his batting were strength and length of hitting, for on one occasion, he hit that most restrictive of bowlers, South African Trevor Goddard, for two sixes – and in a Test match!

As a bowler, he bowled in two styles – orthodox, round-the-wicket slow left-arm and medium over the wicket 'seam-up' and cutters: but occasionally, he would insert one of the either in a spell of the other, and was known to insert a Chinaman into both.

He made his deepest mark on cricket as a fieldsman, formerly at short-leg and then at slip. Always alert and fierce in concentration, he stood as close to the bat as anyone in the history of the game. He would rank with the best of any generation and he fully deserved to amass the fourth highest total of catches by a fielder with an entirely post-war career. Against Middlesex at Lord's in 1962, he was on the field of play for all three days, except 45 minutes. He was pressed into service as an emergency opening batsman against an attack including Alan Moss and Fred Titmus. He batted through the innings for an unbeaten 152 and then took seven for 58 with the new ball!

At the end of the 1962 season he left Glamorgan with the intention of settling in South Africa, but his wife's health could not accept the climate. In June 1963, Walker rejoined the Club, having missed the competitive thrust of county cricket, also taking up a journalist's post with a television company in Cardiff.

Walker was tipped to be the County's new captain in 1973, but the 1972 season had ended on a sour note for the all-rounder, as he was out of form and dropped for the last match at Worcester. He was reluctant to sign a new contract and decided that his future lay in journalism and on 2nd March 1973, he wrote to the Club officially resigning.

A man of many talents, Peter Walker is remembered in Glamorgan for his ability to take the barely perceptible half-chance and make it look like just another simple catch.

CYRIL WALTERS

Born: 28th August, 1905. Bedlinog
Died: 23rd December, 1992
Played: 1923-1928

FIRST-CLASS GLAMORGAN RECORD

Innings	Not Out	Runs
133	9	2146
H.Sc.	Average	100's
116	17.31	2

Overs	Mdns	Runs	Wkts	Average	Best
5.2	0	37	0	–	–

NOTABLE FEATS
- He scored his maiden first-class century for Glamorgan, 116 v. Warwickshire at Swansea in 1926.
- For Worcestershire, he exceeded 1,000 runs in a season on 5 occasions with a best of 2,165 runs in 1933 – then a County record. It was also the season in which he made his highest score for the County, 226 v. Kent at Gravesend.
- He scored 784 runs at Test level at an average of 52.26.

AN ELEGANT OPENING BATSMAN, Cyril Walters left Glamorgan in 1928 to become secretary of Worcersteshire, whom he captained from 1931 to 1935.

As a schoolboy he had a most impressive record and was selected for the County team in 1923 after a number of outstanding innings made under the watchful eye of 'Tal' Whittington.

It was the summer of 1926 when Walters scored his maiden first-class century for Glamorgan, as the County recorded their seventh success of the season against Warwickshire at Swansea. Batting first they totalled 336 with Cyril Walters hitting 116 and adding 113 for the fourth wicket with Johnny Clay in the process. His other hundred for Glamorgan came later in the season when Leicestershire provided the opposition. At lunch-time on the last day, Glamorgan were within 24 runs of victory with four wickets in hand, but on resuming, Cyril Walters on 114 not out had the mortification of seeing all four men leave for the addition of only nine runs. Although Glamorgan were set to get the highest innings of the match to win, the game was there for the taking. Also during this season he hit 69 against both Somerset at Weston-super-Mare and Yorkshire at Swansea to finish second in the County's averages with 694 runs at 34.70.

He started the following season in fine form, hitting 78 in the opening match against Esssex at Leyton and followed it by top scoring in both innings of the next match against Yorkshire at Cardiff (39* out of 83 and 20 out of 120). After six matches in which he proved himself to be one of the most reliable bats in the team (303 runs at 30.30) he dropped a bombshell by announcing his retirement, albeit temporarily from cricket for business reasons.

He later announced that he would be returning to cricket, but with Worcestershire and was taking the Secretary's post with his adopted county.

In 1931 when he qualified, he took over the captaincy of the Worcestershire side and his brilliant batsmanship was soon to reveal itself. He played an innings of 157 not out against Northants and the following year scored 1,500 runs to head the batting averages. By 1933 he was the finest opening batsman in England and began the season by maing 226 against Kent at Gravesend. For Worcestershire that summer he scored 2,165 runs – a new County record. He played three Tests against the West Indies in 1933 and went to India with Jardine's side the following winter.

Selected for the first Test against Australia in 1934, a year in which Wisden chose him as one of the Five Cricketers of the Year, he suddenly found himself captain when Wyatt withdrew with a broken thumb. The only other amateurs in the side were Farnes and the Nawab of Pataudi. Though professionals of the experience of Ames, Hammond, Hendren, Sutcliffe and Verity were playing, such were the ethics of the time that they could not be considered for the captaincy.

In 1934 he had another wonderful season for both his county and his country and 1935 saw two hundreds from his magical bat before he gave up the first-class game to the surprise and regret of many cricket followers.

STEVE WATKIN

Born: 15th September, 1964. Duffryn, Rhondda, nr. Port Talbot
Played: 1986-

FIRST-CLASS GLAMORGAN RECORD

Innings	Not Out	Runs	H.Sc.	Average	100's
157	56	1100	41	10.89	–

Overs	Mdns	Runs	Wkts	Average	Best
5098.0	1095	15173	528	28.73	8-59

NOTABLE FEATS
- He took 8 for 59 v. Warwickshire at Edgbaston in 1988.
- In 1989, he was the country's leading wicket taker with 94 wickets at 25.10.

THERE CAN HARDLY BE a more reliable, less-trumpeted old-fashioned quickish bowler then Steve Watkin.

The new-ball bowler from a former tin-mining community in Rhondda, had marked himself down as an interesting prospect by taking 46 first-class wickets in 1988, though he had made his County debut some two years earlier. At Edgbaston that season, he produced the best figures of his career, eight for 59 in Warwickshire's first innings in what was the County's sole championship victory.

He confirmed the impression with ten wickets against Leicestershire in the opening game of the 1989 season and played the decisive part in Glamorgan's first win of that season at Swansea by reducing Northamptonshire to six for five, a forlorn start towards a target of 305. Watkin got six for 42 that day. He soon had 13 wickets in a match (7 for 65 and 6 for 94) as, on an excellent cricket wicket at Old Trafford, Glamorgan ended Lancashire's challenge nine runs short and with just one ball to spare!

It was performances like these that brought Watkin to wider attention and prompted the inevitable question about his ambitions to play for England, but it was two seasons later before these were realised.

Watkin ended that summer of 1989 as the country's leading wicket taker with 94 wickets at 25.10 runs apiece, and was instrumental in Glamorgan winning their three Championship games.

Although he was unlucky not to tour the West Indies, his efforts were rewarded with a place in the England 'A' team to tour Zimbabwe.

The only time the popular bowler allows himself to bowl fast is at tailenders! But to opening batsmen, he prefers to try and hit the seam, to maintain line and length and to 'work batsmen out rather than blast them out'.

A graduate in Human Movement Studies, his time at the South Glamorgan Institute taught him about the temperament of physical activity and he learned not to get rattled if he bowled a bad over or get hit. He can even tell you that 'the bowlers front foot comes down at seven times the normal force of running'.

Making his Test debut against the West Indies at Headingley in June 1991, Watkins' first victim was Desmond Haynes as the opening batsman edged his outswinger to Jack Russell. In the second innings, he swung the match England's way with three wickets in consecutive overs of generously-pitched bowling – Hooper nicked to slip; Richards, after only 10 minutes at the crease, sent a terrifying skier way over Gooch, who took it over his shoulder at deep mid-off and then Logie who was caught by Gooch off a thick edge.

During the County's run in the limelight in 1993, captain Hugh Morris paid due credit to the massive contribution of Steve Watkin. He was recalled to the England side for the sixth and final Test match against Australia at the Oval, where he was (along with Matthew Maynard) one of two Glamorgan players in the final XI – the first time the County had supplied this number.

After taking 2 for 87 in the first innings, his first delivery on the final day slipped from his fingers and rolled out to cover point. Slater strolling across, whacked the ball for four to the Bedser Stand. Watkin then took two wickets with consecutive balls – Slater off his forearm and Boon l.b.w. – Waugh averted the hat-trick. In his next over, he bowled Taylor off the inside edge to clinch 3 for 3 in seven balls. He later dismissed Healy, caught by Maynard – the long-legged, splay-footed Watkins now had four wickets and had contributed handsomely to an England victory by 161 runs.

Prior to the 1993 season, Watkin lived up to his nickname of 'Banger'. Having picked up his new sponsored BMW, courtesy of Eagle Executive, he proceeded within a matter of days, to all but write it off. Bemoaning his luck and a £6,000 bill, he said afterwards that he had been blinded by the sun (surely not a problem often faced by cricketers in Wales!) – quite ironic then that in *The Cricketers Who's Who*, he lists under relaxations 'motor mechanics' and under opinions on cricket, 'travelling must be cut down for the sake of safety'! After topping the Glamorgan bowling averages in 1994 and 1995, the latter season taking 65 wickets at 27.00 each and a best of 7 for 49, Steve Watkin will be looking to improve on those figures this summer and regain his place in the England side for the Test series against India and Pakistan.

ALLAN WATKINS

Born: 12st April, 1922. Usk
Played: 1939-1962

FIRST-CLASS GLAMORGAN RECORD

Innings	Not Out	Runs
649	76	17419
H.Sc.	Average	100's
170*	30.30	29

Overs	Mdns	Runs	Wkts	Average	Best
7397.5	2027	17683	774	22.84	7-28

NOTABLE FEATS
- He took four wickets with five successive balls v. Derbyshire at Chesterfield in 1954.
- He scored 1,000 runs in a season for Glamorgan on 13 occasions.
- In 1955, he did the 'double' with 1,114 runs at 24.22 and 113 wickets at 20.09.
- He held 390 catches in his career with Glamorgan.

ALLAN WATKINS WAS A FINE county cricketer. A considerable all-rounder, he was an attacking yet solid left-handed batsman and an effective and often unplayble left-arm medium paced bowler. No less an authority than E. W. Swanton describes him as 'the best short leg I have ever seen'.

Born at Usk on 21st April 1922, he made his first-class debut in 1939, and scored his maiden century in 1946 against Surrey at the Arms Park. Going in at 82 for five, he drove fiercely through the covers on a wicket giving some assistance to the bowlers. Only one Surrey batsman exceeded fifty, as Glamorgan made them follow-on, before winning by nine wickets. In fact, Watkins had been a last minute choice, for he should have been at pre-season training with Plymouth Argyle F.C., for whom he played during the winter months.

He was in fine form the following summer, scoring 1,407 runs at 33.50, including five centuries. He hit 146 in the drawn match with Northants at Kettering and followed it with a first day 111 against Worcestershire at Ebbw Vale – a drawn game ended with Glamorgan within reach of victory, only three Worcestershire wickets being left standing with 44 runs needed for victory. At Weston-super-Mare, he scored 105 as he and George Lavis (87) made a fine stand for the third wicket, victory being achieved with four wickets in hand. His final century of the summer, 110, came in the four wicket win over Surrey at Cardiff.

He proved a key member of Glamorgan's first Championship-winning side in 1948 under Wilf Wooller. In the same year, he became the first Glamorgan player to represent England against Australia, when he was picked for the fifth Test at the Oval. It wasn't a baptism he enjoys recalling. England were routed for 52 by a rampant Ray Lindwall who not only took six wickets, but rendered Watkins a blow on the shoulder as he was dismissed for a duck.

He then had to retire to the pavilion after opening the bowling with Alec Bedser. The injury crippled him for the rest of the match and forced him to miss the historic game at Bournemouth which took the Championship. He was chosen to tour South Africa with the M.C.C. in 1948-49 and after half-centuries against Griqualand and Transvaal, he was chosen for the first Test at Durban. Though he only made 9 and 4 and failed to take a wicket, he impressed with his fielding, and this kept him in the side for the rest of the series. In the fourth Test at Johannesburg, he became the first Glamorgan player to score a century in Test cricket. He batted for a long time with Denis Compton, who played the South African spinners with great skill. Watkins asked him if he was nervous and Compton's reply was: 'A man who is not nervous is not worth his place'. Watkins was on 90 when Compton's county colleague, last man, Jack Young, came to the wicket, but the spinner gave him good support and after $3\frac{1}{2}$ hours batting he reached three figures. Though he had a reputation for being calm, Watkins confessed to smoking like a chimney and suffering from nerves throughout this tour! On his return, he was England twelfth man against New Zealand at Leeds and played at Lord's, but was then surprisingly passed over until his selection for the 1951-52 M.C.C. tour of India.

In 1951, he finished the season as the County's leading run-getter with 1,557 runs besides taking 61 wickets and 37 catches, and was rewarded with selection for the M.C.C. tour of India, Pakistan and Ceylon. His aggregate on that tour was 451 runs at an average of 64.42. At Delhi in the first Test, he batted for $9\frac{1}{2}$ hours to score 137 and save England from defeat, becoming in the process the first England player to bat throughout the day of a Test in India. In fact, he was so tired towards the end of his innings that his knees buckled and he sank to the ground as one of the Indians was about to bowl! He ended up playing out time with Hampshire's Derek Shackleton, who wasn't the worst bat in a situation like that, the two of them taking ends to save the match.

He played 15 times for England, scoring 810 runs, averaging 40.50 with two centuries.

The following summer, he scored 1,135 runs and captured 84 wickets. His all-round form was never more evident than in the match against Leicestershire at Neath. His medium fast-swing bowling enabling him to take five for 16, whilst his adventurous middle-order play brought him a sparkling 107.

In 1954, he took four wickets in five balls for Glamorgan against Derbyshire at Chesterfield, whilst achieving the 'double' for the first time. He repeated the achievement the following season, hitting 170 against Leicestershire and taking seven for 28 against Derbyshire – his 113 wickets were gained from over 950 overs of either fast left-arm seam or slower cutters, depending on the wicket.

He eventually announced his retirement from the first-class

game in June 1962 after twenty-three years of county cricket. He had been troubled by asthma and a stomach complaint and after the match against Kent at Gravesend, he decided to take a warder's post at Usk Borstal. Overall, he made 20,362 runs at an average of 30.57, including 32 centuries and took 833 wickets at an average of 24.48. He also notched up 461 catches.

His arrival at Oundle School in 1971 occurred as a result of Wilf Wooller's son being placed under the care of Michael Mills, a housemaster at the school. Donald Carr had found Watkins a job at Framlingham College and when Arnold Dyson was ready to retire at Oundle, Mills approached Watkins through Wilf Wooller to see if he was interested.

Allan Watkins was cricket coach at Oundle School from 1971 to 1988 before continuing to lend a helping hand with the colts teams. He was a great believer in coaching the ability of each boy and he must have been very proud of the manner and technique with which his charges played the game – as he did in his days with Glamorgan.

OSSIE WHEATLEY

Born: 28th May, 1935. Low Fell, Gateshead
Played: 1961-1970

FIRST-CLASS GLAMORGAN RECORD

Innings	Not Out	Runs	H.Sc.	Average	100's
227	87	799	30	5.70	0

Overs	Mdns	Runs	Wkts	Average	Best
6262.2	1988	13356	715	18.67	9-60

NOTABLE FEATS
- He took 100 wickets in a season for Glamorgan on 3 occasions.
- In 1962, he took 133 wickets at 18.57 runs each.
- He performed the hat-trick v. Somerset at Taunton in 1968.

- He took nine for 60 v. Sussex at Ebbw Vale in 1968.
- He holds the Glamorgan record for the best first-class bowling average – taking 82 wickets at 12.95 runs each in 1968.

A FORMER CAMBRIDGE BLUE, Ossie Wheatley spent four years playing for Warwickshire, before eventually agreeing terms with Glamorgan. He had impressed the Welsh Club's officials by taking nine wickets against them in the match at Edgbaston and he agreed to accept a business appointment in South Wales.

Ossie Wheatley captained Glamorgan for six years from 1961 to 1966 inclusively and played periodically for another few years under the leadership of Tony Lewis.

He became the first person outside the Principality to lead Glamorgan in the County Championship on a regular basis – there were four poor and two very good years. He had a difficult first year in charge due to injury and illness, but still managed to turn in match figures of 13 for 115 in the match against Leicestershire at Grace Road and take 100 wickets for the first time.

In 1962 he captured 126 wickets in Championship matches alone at 18.71 with a best of seven for 55. The following year, Glamorgan finished second to Yorkshire in the County Championship, winning 11 of their 28 matches. That they lost 8 matches was simply due to the fact that Ossie Wheatley was a captain who always took a chance and liked to make a good game of cricket by declaring. He was a man who led by personal example, who never stinted himself yet was always open to an alternative viewpoint put by one of his side.

In 1965 he sued successfully, the *Daily Express* and *Daily Sketch* for libel after they implied that by turning up to toss at Colchester for the match against Essex in a dinner jacket, Wheatley had attended an all-night party and was in no fit state to play cricket – but in fact, he and Tony Lewis had attended the Hawks Club Dinner in London the evening before and did not have any other casual clothes apart from their whites!

The following year, he took 103 wickets at 15.94 with a best of six for 27 to finish fifth in the national first-class bowling averages – it was the third occasion that he'd taken over one hundred wickets for the County.

Ossie Wheatley was a fierce competitor with one of the shrewdest cricketing brains of his time. The spirit and attitude he instilled into the Glamorgan team which he handed over to Tony Lewis led to the County winning the Championship in 1969.

He had another outstanding year in 1968, taking 82 wickets at 12.95, giving a much needed boost to a flagging Glamorgan attack. His nine for 60 against Sussex at Ebbw Vale was the best performance of his career. Also that summer he performed the only hat-trick of his career in the match against Somerset at Taunton.

A man with a great sense of humour, I remember in 1969 attending a televised game at Southport when Lancashire were chasing just 113 runs to win in a Sunday League game. Farohk Engineer hit an unbeaten 78 in flamboyant style as Lancashire won by nine wickets. Opening the bowling, Ossie was heard to say: 'I don't mind him charging, but I do wish he would let me set off first.'

Also that season in one of his rare appearances for the County in the Championship, he sprinted round the boundary and returned an arrow-like throw over the top of the stumps and into Eifion Jones's gloves. He triumphantly removed the bails and Essex's John Lever was well out of his ground to give Glamorgan victory by one run!

The year of 1969 was his penultimate one in the Welsh Club's colours – Wheatley taking 715 wickets at 18.67 runs in his time at Glamorgan. Ossie was appointed Club Chairman in 1977, but with business commitments taking more and more of his time, he had to rely increasingly on the day by day availability of Bill Edwards and so, in 1983, he relinquished the post.

His contribution to the continuation of county cricket in Wales and its improving future was as substantial as his playing achievements on the field. In fact, Ossie's contribution to Glamorgan – first as a Captain and then as Chairman is a difficult one to equal.

'TAL' WHITTINGTON

Born: 29th July, 1881. Neath
Died: 19th July, 1944
Played: 1901-1923

FIRST-CLASS GLAMORGAN RECORD

Innings	Not Out	Runs	H.Sc.	Average	100's
218	11	4563	188	22.04	4

Overs	Mdns	Runs	Wkts	Average	Best
7.5	1	53	3	17.647	3-26

NOTABLE FEATS
- He made his top score of 188 against Carmarthenshire at Llanelli in 1908.
- He was the man who helped secure first-class recognition for Glamorgan.

AS J. H. MORGAN WROTE, 'the name of 'Tal' Whittington will always be identified with the history of Glamorgan C.C.C. as he did more than any other individual to secure Glamorgan's promotion to first-class status.'

'Tal' Whittington's father was a doctor in Neath and a very useful sportsman, having played rugby for Scotland as well as for J. T. D.

Llewellyn's Glamorganshire side on several occasions in the 1860s and 1870s.

'Tal' made his Glamorgan debut as an 18-year-old batsman in 1901 and after leaving Oxford University, appeared regularly for the County. He soon began to establish himself as a top order batsman, with a wide range of attractive strokes. He headed the Glamorgan averages in 1908 with 44.23, making his top score of 188 in the match against Carmarthenshire at Llanelli.

Whittington was appointed as the honorary secretary in 1909, and took over from Brain as the Club's captain. He had a solicitor's practice and used his wide range of contacts in the commercial world to drum up financial support, for he realised that the main stumbling block to the Club's aspirations was the absence of capital reserves allowing the Club to play 16 fixtures (home and away) and commit themselves to all the other expenses of regular county cricket.

The only bright note at the end of the 1910 season, when he scored 600 runs at 42.85, was his selection for the M.C.C. tour to the West Indies. The Welsh County's captain had a fine tour, topping the batting averages with 685 runs at 34.01, including a magnificent 154 against British Guiana and an unbeaten 115 in the match with All Jamaica.

Returning to South Wales he was soon brought down to earth because the financial situation of the Club had deteriorated. The earlier promises of financial support went out of the window, and so Whittington met with the Earl of Plymouth for a second time to draft a circular to businesses in the community in a final effort to avert the unthinkable step of withdrawing from the competition. Given these financial worries, the Club were very fortunate in being allowed to stage a game between a South Wales XI and the All-Indian tourists at the Arms Park. Whittington's contacts within the hierarchy of the M.C.C. were a good help and he led the South Wales side to a seven wicket victory, with the Neath solicitor paving the way in the second innings as they chased 81 for the win.

In 1912 he was appointed captain of the Minor County team which met the South African tourists at Stoke and at the end of the season went on the M.C.C. tour of the West Indies. During that season he was the only Glamorgan batsman in form. There was plenty of pressure on Whittington in the match with Staffordshire in August. Near the end of the match, which was heading towards yet another defeat for the Welsh team, he got involved in a row with the umpires. At the end of the summer, he felt it was time to stand down as captain, and he handed over the leadership to Norman Riches.

He was now able to devote more of his time to his duties as Secretary and easing the Club's cash problems.

In 1920, he captained the Minor Counties in their annual match against the M.C.C. – he had showed good form that summer, scoring 76 not out in the County's opening match, a dramatic win over Surrey II. At the end of the season, in which the County finished sixth, he was encouraged by the new faces and results to continue his pursuit of securing first-class status.

During the autumn of 1920, the Glamorgan committee unanimously agreed that 'Tal' Whittington should be the person to seek the support of the other counties. He travelled the length and breadth of England persuading other officials that Glamorgan was equipped both on and off the field to enter the first-class game. Whittington reported back to the committee in November that he had secured the support of seven counties. The committee were understandably jubilant with their target in sight and told him 'to obtain the eighth at any cost whatsoever'. Strong persuasion was not needed and at the December meeting, Whittington was able to announce that the required number of fixtures had been obtained. Whittington also gained assurances from businessmen in Cardiff and Swansea that they would write off the Club's deficit of £350 if Glamorgan gained the M.C.C.'s approval at the turn of the year. A few weeks later, the M.C.C. endorsed the Club's application – and at the 1921 A.G.M. he was elected as the first life member of the Club in recognition of his efforts.

It was very appropriate that Whittington and Riches (another playing a leading role) should open the batting in the first match against Sussex at the Arms Park.

Whittington began to lose form as a batsman and moved down the order in 1922 and 1923 to accommodate more youngsters. He averaged only 14.61 in 1923 and decided that it was the right time to retire. The Glamorgan committee reluctantly accepted his resignation as captain, realising that the tragic death of Brock Williams, a close friend who had persuaded his colleagues in the business world to support the Club, had also influenced his decision. Whittington decided to leave South Wales and took a teaching post at Lancing College.

A shrewd reader of the game, he had a good sense of humour and as the Club met with many problems in the 1920s, he took all the criticism with a wry smile and an optimistic word about the future.

WILF WOOLLER

Born: 20th November, 1912. Rhos-on-Sea
Played: 1938-1962

FIRST-CLASS GLAMORGAN RECORD

Innings	Not Out	Runs	H.Sc.	Average	100's
630	72	12692	128	22.75	5

Overs	Mdns	Runs	Wkts	Average	Best
9118.5	2332	23513	887	26.50	8-45

NOTABLE FEATS
- He shares the Glamorgan 7th wicket record partnership with W. E. Jones – 195* v. Lancashire at Liverpool in 1947.
- He did the 'double' in 1954, scoring 1,059 runs at 24.06 and taking 107 wickets at 18.42 each.
- He took 100 wickets in a season for Glamorgan on two occasions.
- He took 392 catches in his career with Glamorgan.

AS CAPTAIN, PLAYER AND ADMINISTRATOR, Wilf Wooller gave Glamorgan wonderful service. In a playing career which stretched from 1938 to 1962, he scored 12,692 runs, took 887 wickets and held 392 catches. He completed the 'double' of 1,000 runs and 100 wickets in 1954 and one of the greatest periods of his colourful cricketing career was to lead Glamorgan to their first Championship title in 1948.

Learning his cricket in North Wales, Wilf Wooller played first for Rydal School, then Denbighshire. After winning two Blues at Cambridge, he moved to South Wales to work, finding little time to play cricket. Eventually, after some excellent all-round performances for St Fagan's, which impressed Jack Mercer, who had seen him play in North Wales and knew that Lancashire had offered him terms, he made his debut for Glamorgan. It was Maurice Turnbull, his former rugby team-mate for Cardiff, who persuaded him to play for the County.

During the season of 1939, he was awarded his County cap and hit his maiden first-class century, 111 in the Bank Holiday match against the West Indies, though the tourists won by two wickets inside two days.

During the war, he served in the Army – the greatest anxiety at the time was felt for Wilf Wooller, who had been in Java in early 1942, and no news was received from him after the Japanese had overrun the Far East. The anxiety was relieved when news finally came through that he was a prisoner in Japanese hands.

It is said that when Wilfred Wooller played his first match after his repatriation from the Japanese prison camp and went out to the wicket, tears were running down the cheeks of grown men. But it would have taken more than the Japanese to daunt Wilf Wooller – 'We played a game at Changi prison camp in Singapore on Christmas Day. Somehow we found a ball and a bat and made some stumps. We had an England versus Australia Test match right there in front of the Japanese guards. They looked puzzled.'

His was the sad, but familiar story of a return from years of captivity and privation, only to find that life had changed behind his back. It was in Africa that a frightening adventure in a crash-landing airplane, made him realise that life was still precious. Wilf decided to do something with his and returned to South Wales to become captain of a Glamorgan team that was to make history.

As a captain, he always led from the front and was never afraid to ask anyone to do a thing he himself would not think twice about – in fact, Wilf Wooller was ready to do anything in his side's best interest, be it opening the batting or bowling, or fielding at short-leg.

When runs were badly wanted he would get them, as in the 1948 match against Surrey when, after Glamorgan's first wicket had painstakingly collected 91, Wooller, by tremendous driving and cutting, hit 89, and only one other batsman scored more than six. In bowling that summer, he performed no spectacular feats, but you couldn't have sent down nearly 900 overs and take 66 wickets without having impressed his personality upon a number of batsmen and broken a number of resistances which made all the difference to the game. As for the fielding machine, he invented it, and was an essential part of it. In the two matches which had the most critical bearing on the Championship, it was catching that finally settled the matter. In one match, Cliff held six catches and in another Watkins held five. At Trent Bridge against Notts, Parkhouse held four in the first innings. Somebody under his captain's guidance must have been awake somewhere!

Like all personalities, stories surround Wilf Wooller. Legend has it that he and 'Sam' Cook of Gloucestershire had a gentle skirmish! Following-on, Glamorgan were not doing too well. Cook had created havoc in the first innings, taking seven wickets and in the second had taken five more when Wilf came in to bat. As he passed 'Sam' he said: 'I bet you would love to bowl against this lot of clowns every day, wouldn't you?' As Wilf prepared to receive his first ball, it turned, lifted and gloved him and the catch was easily taken. Trudging back to the pavilion, 'Sam' called out to him: 'Good afternoon, Mr Ring Master!' – I'm sure Wilf would have enjoyed that exchange!

Wilf also enjoyed the odd exchange with the umpires! During the period when teams could only have five fielders on the leg-side and only one behind the wicket, Wilf was bowling with two short-leg fielders. So Harry Baldwin, a little character of an umpire, decided to move to point for a better view. Suddenly, he cried out 'No Ball!' For a moment, the crowd and players thought he had called him for throwing. When Wooller enquired what the 'No-Ball' was for, Harry, sticking his finger behind his braces and pushing his chest full out, retorted 'Six men on the leg-side skipper'. 'You what!' cried the irate Glamorgan skipper, 'where are they?' Harry burst forth: 'Mid-on, mid-wicket, two short-legs, square-leg and fine leg.' Wilf spluttered and then erupted: 'Fine-leg! You daft ... that's an ice-cream man down there!'

In 1954 at the age of 41, Wooller achieved the 'double' for the only time in his career. When he passed both the 1,000 runs and 100 wicket mark, which happened in the match with Warwickshire at Edgbaston, when he claimed his 100th wicket, the Warwickshire chairman, Alec Hastilow walked out to the wicket with a tray of vintage champagne and drank a glass with Wilf to celebrate becoming the first (and only) Glamorgan amateur to achieve the feat.

After retiring in 1960 (though he did come out of retirement for one game in 1962) he played a leading role in the Club's affairs, acting as Secretary until 1978. A major force behind the modern development of the Welsh Club, he is now President of Glamorgan.

Wilf 'fought' everybody, including the Japanese, if he thought it was right, and there is no doubt he has made some enemies; but even they, at least the fair minded, could not help but respect him.

APPENDICES

STATISTICAL ANALYSIS

SELECTING A BEST TEAM ever can be a fascinating relaxation, but it can also be highly provocative. For players were at their best in different decades and comparisons can be odious, and the more one thinks of all the players who have represented Glamorgan, the more difficult the task of selecting the best eleven becomes.

For whilst it is purely a matter of opinion as to how good a player a man is or has been, and it is certainly true that figures seldom tell the true story of any cricketer, I hope the following will go some way to explaining why I have chosen the following eleven players as my team of 'Famous Cricketers of Glamorgan' though it wasn't easy to leave out players of the calibre of Tony Lewis, Jack Mercer, Viv Richards, Peter Walker and Wilf Wooller.

1. Alan Jones
2. Gilbert Parkhouse
3. Emrys Davies
4. Javed Miandad
5. Majid Khan
6. Maurice Turnbull
7. Allan Watkins
8. Haydn Davies
9. Don Shepherd
10. Johnny Clay
11. Jeff Jones

GLAMORGAN TOP TENS

THE FOLLOWING SECTION lists the best performances in each of several categories, showing in statistical form the 'Top Ten' for Glamorgan.

MOST MATCHES

1.	D. J. Shepherd	647
2.	D. E. Davies	612
3.	A. Jones	610
4.	P. M. Walker	437
5.	W. G. A. Parkhouse	435
6.	H. G. Davies	423
7.	B. Hedges	422
8.	A. H. Dyson	412
	J. Mercer	412
10.	D. Davies	411

MOST RUNS

1.	A. Jones	34056
2.	D. E. Davies	26102
3.	W. G. A. Parkhouse	22619
4.	A. H. Dyson	17920
5.	B. Hedges	17733
6.	A. J. Watkins	17419
7.	P. M. Walker	16510
8.	D. Davies	15008
9.	A. R. Lewis	15003
10.	M. J. L. Turnbull	14431

MOST WICKETS

1.	D. J. Shepherd	2174
2.	J. Mercher	1460
3.	J. C. Clay	1292
4.	H. Creber	1225
5.	M. A. Nash	991
6.	F. P. Ryan	913
7.	W. Wooller	887
8.	D. E. Davies	885
9.	J. E. McConnon	799
10.	A. J. Watkins	774

MOST CATCHES
(Fieldsmen)

1.	P. M. Walker	656
2.	W. Wooller	392
3.	A. J. Watkins	390
4.	J. S. Pressdee	344
5.	W. G. A. Parkhouse	312
6.	A. Jones	276
7.	M. J. L. Turnbull	253
8.	D. J. Shepherd	241
9.	D. E. Davies	211
10.	J. A. Hopkins	210

MOST HUNDREDS

1.	A. Jones	52
2.	H. Morris	37
3.	W. G. A. Parkhouse	32
4.	D. E. Davies	31
5.	A. J. Watkins	29
6.	A. H. Dyson	24
	M. P. Paynard	24
8.	M. J. L. Turnbull	22
9.	B. Hedges	21
	A. R. Lewis	21
	Majid Khan	21

MOST INTERNATIONAL APPEARANCES

1.	I. V. A. Richards	121
2.	Javed Miandad	114
3.	R. J. Shastri	73
4.	Majid Khan	63
5.	R. C. Fredericks	59
6.	I. J. Jones	15
	A. J. Watkins	15
8.	A. R. Lewis	9
	M. J. L. Turnbull	9
10.	W. G. A. Parkhouse	7

BATTING AVERAGES

1.	Javed Miandad	57.80
2.	I. V. A. Richards	45.45
3.	A. R. Butcher	44.65
4.	R. J. Shastri	42.49
6.	M. P. Maynard	41.87
5.	R. C. Fredericks	41.54
8.	H. Morris	38.62
7.	Majid Khan	37.98
9.	N. V. H. Riches	36.18
10.	A. Jones	33.03

BOWLING AVERAGES

1.	A. Nash	15.56
2.	A. D. G. Matthews	15.88
3.	H. Creber	15.98
4.	O. S. Wheatley	18.67
5.	J. C. Clay	19.49
6.	J. E. McConnon	19.59
7.	B. L. Muncer	20.42
8.	F. P. Ryan	20.86
9.	D. J. Shepherd	20.95
10.	J. S. Pressdee	22.18

There are other players with better bowling averages, but they haven't been included, as they haven t either played enough matches or performed as a regular bowler to warrant inclusion.

HIGHEST SCORES

1.	D. E. Davies	287*	v. Gloucestershire at Newport	1939
2.	M. P. Maynard	243	v. Hampshire at Southampton	1991
3.	M. J. L. Turnbull	233	v. Worcestershire at Swansea	1937
4.	J. A. Hopkins	230	v. Worcestershire at Worcester	1977
5.	R. C. Fredericks	228*	v. Northamptonshire at Swansea	1972
6.	I. V. A. Richards	224*	v. Middlesex at Cardiff	1993
7.	A. R. Lewis	223	v. Kent at Gravesend	1966
8.	N. V. H. Riches	217*	v. Dorset at Blandford	1907
9.	D. Davies	216	v. Somerset at Newport	1939
10.	Javed Miandad	212*	v. Leicestershire at Swansea	1984
	W. E. Jones	212*	v. Essex at Brentwood	1948

Also scored

D. E. Davies	215	v. Essex at Brentwood	1948

The following would normally figure in the 'Top Ten' but haven't been included, as they have not been classed as Famous Glamorgan Cricketers.

R. J. Duckfield	280*	v. Surrey at the Oval	1936
H. E. Morgan	254	v. Monmouthshire at Arms Park	1901
J. T. Bell	225	v. Worcestershire at Dudley	1926

BATTING AVERAGES

Up to the end of the 1995 Season

	Inns	No's	Runs	H.Sc.	Averages	100's
T. Arnott	321	25	4726	153	15.96	3
W. J. Bancroft	358	20	8353	157	24.71	7
W. E. Bates	510	15	12802	200*	25.86	10
J. H. Brain	223	18	5283	144	25.77	4
A. R. Butcher	190	17	7795	171*	45.05	17
J. C. Clay	536	88	6868	115*	15.33	2
P. B. Clift	306	21	6055	125*	21.24	7
A. E. Cordle	433	76	5239	81	14.67	0
H. Creber	300	108	1779	52	9.27	0
D. Davies	681	61	15008	216	24.20	16
D. E. Davies	1016	79	26102	287*	27.85	31
H. G. Davies	596	95	6515	80	13.00	0
R. C. Davis	369	30	7363	134	21.71	5

– *Famous Cricketers of Glamorgan* –

	Inns	*No's*	*Runs*	*H.Sc.*	*Averages*	*100's*
A. H. Dyson	696	37	17920	208	27.19	24
D. G. L. Evans	364	91	2875	46*	10.53	0
R. C. Fredericks	80	8	2991	228*	41.54	7
B. Hedges	744	41	17733	182	25.22	21
J. A. Hopkins	524	32	13610	230	27.66	18
Javed Miandad	135	22	6531	212*	57.80	17
A. Jones	1102	71	34056	204*	33.03	52
E. W. Jones	591	119	8341	146*	17.67	3
I. J. Jones	180	69	395	20	3.55	0
W. E. Jones	555	63	13270	212*	27.00	11
G. Lavis	312	43	4957	154	18.42	3
A. R. Lewis	546	52	15003	223	30.37	21
J. E. McConnon	350	38	4514	95	14.70	0
Majid Khan	270	17	9610	204	37.98	21
A. D. G. Matthews	71	24	691	37	14.70	0
M. P. Maynard	334	33	12603	243	41.87	24
J. Mercer	578	100	5730	72	11.98	0
H. Morris	414	42	14370	166*	38.62	37
B. L. Muncer	333	46	6460	135	22.50	4
A. Nash	225	45	1302	44	7.20	0
M. A. Nash	467	67	7120	130	17.81	2
R. C. Ontong	413	65	10825	204*	31.10	18
W. G. A. Parkhouse	759	48	22619	201	31.81	32
J. S. Pressdee	543	83	13411	150*	29.16	12
I. V. A. Richards	82	10	3273	224*	45.45	9
N. V. H. Riches	362	28	11722	217*	36.18	20
F. P. Ryan	312	100	1699	46	8.01	0
R. J. Shastri	99	18	3442	157	42.49	6
D. J. Shepherd	816	214	5610	73	9.75	0
C. C. Smart	301	35	8069	151*	3034	9
J. G. Thomas	139	24	2137	110	18.58	2
M. J. L. Turnbull	504	25	14431	233	30.12	22
P. M. Walker	738	106	16510	152*	26.12	12
C. F. Walters	133	9	2146	116	17.31	2
S. L. Watkin	157	56	1100	41	10.89	0
A. J. Watkins	649	76	17419	170*	30.39	29
O. S. Wheatley	227	87	799	30	5.70	0
T. A. L. Whittington	218	11	4563	188	22.04	4
W. Wooller	630	72	12692	128	22.75	5

BATTING AVERAGES

185

BOWLING AVERAGES

Up to the end of the 1995 Season

	Overs	Mdns	Runs	Wkts	Averages	Best
T. Arnott	3697.3	642	11435	361	31.68	7-40
W. J. Bancroft	44.1	12	153	9	17.00	3-30
W. E. Bates	2217.4	213	8707	239	36.43	8.93
J. H. Brain	88.4	14	275	19	14.47	6-60
A. R. Butcher	143.4	20	581	13	44.69	3-35
J. C. Clay	9911.1	2326	25181	1292	19.49	9-54
P. B. Clift	216.2	38	675	11	61.36	3-6
A. E. Cordle	7013.5	1615	19281	701	27.50	9-49
H. Creber	7245.0	1776	19570	1225	15.98	9-91
D. Davies	3661.4	774	9404	271	34.70	6-50
D. E. Davies	10264.4	2359	26030	885	29.41	6-24
H. G. Davies	3.0	0	20	1	20.00	1-20
R. C. Davis	2868.0	700	7793	241	32.33	6-62
A. H. Dyson	34.0	2	160	1	160.00	1-9
D. G. L. Evans	4.0	0	12	0	–	–
R. C. Fredericks	207.1	45	667	20	33.35	3-37
B. Hedges	94.0	24	260	3	86.66	1-16
J. A. Hopkins	26.0	3	148	0	–	–
Javed Miandad	254.3	57	851	21	40.52	3-52
A. Jones	58.5	15	249	1	249.00	1-41
E. W. Jones	0.3	0	5	0	–	–
I. J. Jones	3904.4	979	9583	408	23.48	8-11
W. E. Jones	1926.2	438	5620	189	29.73	5-50
G. Lavis	2741.0	515	7768	156	49.79	4-55
A. R. Lewis	55.1	3	306	4	76.50	3-18
J. E. McConnon	5913.2	1593	15656	799	19.59	8-36
Majid Khan	723.3	216	1674	51	32.82	4-48
A. D. G. Matthews	1473.1	352	3607	227	15.88	7-57
M. P. Maynard	99.0	10	478	5	95.60	3-21
J. Mercer	13813.5	3242	34058	1460	23.32	10-51
H. Morris	58.0	6	380	2	190.00	1-6
B. L. Muncer	6642.2	1807	14462	708	20.42	9-62
A. Nash	4969.3	1567	11872	763	15.56	9-93
M. A. Nash	9193.3	2426	25601	991	25.83	9-56
R. C. Ontong	5708.5	1277	17279	531	32.54	8-67
W. G. A. Parkhouse	37.1	8	125	2	62.50	1-4
J. S. Pressdee	3666.2	1095	8988	405	22.18	9-43

	Overs	Mdns	Runs	Wkts	Averages	Best
I. V. A. Richards	149.0	28	460	5	92.00	2-27
N. V. H. Riches	27.3	1	101	1	101.00	1-4
F. P. Ryan	6589.2	1317	19053	913	20.86	8-41
R. J. Shastri	1313.4	341	3264	96	34.00	7-49
D. J. Shepherd	21514.2	7334	45571	2174	20.95	9-47
C. C. Smart	2097.4	302	6943	169	41.08	5-39
J. G. Thomas	2244.5	386	8230	256	32.15	6-68
M. J. L. Turnbull	46.4	2	266	2	133.00	1-4
P. M. Walker	8879.0	2749	21652	771	28.08	7-58
C. F. Walker	5.2	0	37	0	–	–
S. Watkin	5098.0	1095	15173	528	28.73	8-59
A. J. Watkins	7397.5	2027	17683	774	22.84	7-28
O. S. Wheatley	6262.2	1988	13356	715	18.67	9-60
T. A. L. Whittington	7.5	1	53	3	17.67	3-26
W. Wooller	9118.5	2332	23513	887	26.50	8-45

WICKET KEEPING

	Matches	Caught	Stumped	Total	Avr number of victims per match
E. W. Jones	405	840	93	933	2.30
H. G. Davies	423	580	202	782	1.84
D. G. L. Evans	270	503	55	558	2.06

N. V. H. Riches also kept wicket on a number of occasions and made 45 dismissals (39 caught, 6 stumped).

SELECTED BIBLIOGRAPHY

Bailey, Thorn and Wynne-Thomas: *The Who's Who of Cricketers* (Newnes Books 1984)
Glamorgan CCC Yearbooks 1947-95
Benny Greed (ed): *The Wisden Book of Obituaries* (MacDonald Queen Anne 1986)
Andrew Hignell: *The History of Glamorgan CCC* (Christopher Helm 1988)
Christopher Martin-Jenkins: *The Complete Who's Who of Test Cricketers* (Orbis 1980)
J. H. Morgan: *Glamorgan* (Convoy Press 1953)
Playfair Cricket Annual 1951-95
Wayne Thomas: *Glamorgan CCC – The Book of Records* 1921-76 (Davies and Sons (Woking) 1976)
Roy Webber: *Who's Who in World Cricket* (Hodder and Stoughton 1952)
Roy Webber: *County Cricket Championship – a History of the Competition since 1873* (Phoenix Sports Books 1957)
Webber and Arnott: *Glamorgan CCC 1921-47* (The Cricket Book Society 1948)
Wisden Cricketers' Almanac 1898-1995